BF 575 .G7 J69
2001

GAYLORD F

THE PHOENIX
PHENOMENON

THE PHOENIX PHENOMENON

Rising from the Ashes of Grief

JOANNE T. JOZEFOWSKI, Ph.D., R.N.

JASON ARONSON INC.
Northvale, New Jersey
London

This book was set in 11 pt. Century Schoolbook and printed and bound by Book-mart Press, Inc. of North Bergen, NJ.

Library of Congress Cataloging-in-Publication Data

Jozefowski, Joanne T.
    The phoenix phenomenon : rising from the ashes of grief / Joanne
T. Jozefowski.
        p.   cm.
    Includes bibliographical references and index.
    ISBN 0-7657-0209-6
    1. Grief. 2. Bereavement—Psychological aspects. 3. Death—
Psychological aspects. I. Title.
BF575.G7J69 1999
155.9'37—dc21   98–54401

Printed in the United States of America on acid-free paper. For information and catalog write to Jason Aronson Inc., 230 Livingston Street, Northvale, NJ 07647-1726, or visit our website:www.aronson.com

This book is dedicated to my mother,
    Valerie J. (Pluta) Wondolowski,
    whose life is a paradigm of perfect love,

and to my father,
    Dr. Joseph P. Wondolowski (1907–1961),
    Physician, Humanitarian, Dad.

Contents

Foreword

It is fairly easy to sink one's psychological teeth into pathology and to identify problems and trace their possible roots. What is infinitely more complicated, however, is to identify precisely how a person has managed to avoid pathology, or be robustly healthy, especially in situations where there has been significant potential for negative outcomes.

Of course, there is a distinct difference between the absence of pathology or pain and flourishing wellness and healthiness, but in the thanatological literature, this reality appears to have been somewhat overlooked. The traditional focus has been upon negative or neutral outcomes after major loss. Relatively scant attention has been paid to studying the positive responses to bereavement, particularly those that promote growth and transcendence. While most self-help and professional books identify the problems inherent in grieving, too few point out its potentials. Kudos must go to Dr. Joanne T. Jozefowski for illuminating a topic that is so clinically relevant, yet so poorly examined.

For too many authors, as well as for too many bereaved individuals, loss is perceived only in its most negative aspects. There is insufficient appreciation of its positive transformative possibilities. Cure of the grief, elimination of the symptomatology, and survival of the crisis are the goals.

There is a focus on the eradication of distress and a striving for return to prior functioning. And, in truth, there is nothing wrong per se with such objectives. Nevertheless, they fall short of bringing many bereaved individuals to where they want or need to be following the loss of a beloved other. Growth, maturation, meaning making, and numerous other positive outcomes are not only possible, but possible in fashions that have the potential to enhance various aspects of the mourner, honor and connect to the deceased, and contribute to others in the mourner's world.

While the bereaved person may not have had a choice in the death of a loved one, he or she does have a choice in how to respond to that death after the period of acute grief it generates. An individual may stop at survival, may stabilize and work through secondary losses, but not grow past where he or she once was, or may continue on to transcend the experience and surpass that former self.

Healthy contending with the death of a loved one requires active efforts. Merely expressing feelings or reacting to the loss is insufficient. Those, like Jozefowski's Phoenix Grievers, who demonstrate the courage and determination that result in a renaissance of body, mind, and spirit in the aftermath of tragedy, are distinguished from other grievers. The pain and grief for both sets of bereaved individuals are the same, but the responses to it mark the difference between one who survives and one who surpasses, one who only regains former equilibrium and one who grows and transcends the loss.

For those who want to live and not merely survive, for those who want something good and meaningful and constructive to come out of the death of their loved one, for those who desire to achieve self-actualization over simply adequate coping, as well as for those who want to assist them, *The Phoenix Phenomenon: Rising from the Ashes of Grief* is a veritable procedural handbook. Intermingling metaphors, parables, and case examples, Jozefowski delineates the attributes of Phoe-

nix Grievers to provide models for transforming and transcending bereavement and to promote not only healthy growth
but also self-actualization. A developmental roadmap of the
process of grief is accompanied by phase-specific recommendations for the bereaved and for their therapists. Enlightenment and empowerment are the by-products.

Therese A. Rando, Ph.D.
The Institute for the Study and Treatment of Loss
Warwick, Rhode Island
August 1999

Acknowledgments

Most books are neither singular nor solitary projects. They are team efforts, and fortunate is the author who finds the right blend. I was blessed to have superior people by my side and behind me. Without them this book would have remained in its original form, only a dream. My heartfelt thanks and appreciation to my "dream team":

Dr. John Madonna, friend and colleague, who "opened the door" and believed in this book from its inception. His support is immeasurable.

Aldona O. Shumway, whose tireless and unselfish efforts polished and enhanced the manuscript. Her contribution is inestimable.

Dr. Therese A. Rando, colleague and friend, for her ongoing support, enthusiasm, and generous sharing of her time and energy. Terrie is a rare professional whose heart is as bountiful as her talent.

Judith Kowalik, friend and colleague, whose personal and professional expertise contributed a richer texture to the book and whose support has been unlimited.

M. Rachid Och, M.D., friend and colleague, for his wisdom, insight, and dynamic suggestions and for his staunch allegiance and support.

Dr. Al Siebert, friend and colleague, whose professionalism and generosity is exceeded only by his humanitarianism.

Theodore "Ted" Buyniski, longtime supporter, friend, and fellow-writer, who put in many hours of reading and critiquing the manuscript.

Jacqueline N. Gauthier Valle, longtime friend and colleague, whose valuable insights and critique provided an incomparable perspective.

Gloria and Louis Katz, friends beyond measure, who supported, encouraged, and rejoiced in this project.

The Carroll family: Mary, Frank, Lisa, Brian, June, Kathleen, Paul (Featherston) and Kevin, my cheerleaders all the way—Kevin, my godson, who enriched this book through his life and his death.

To my colleagues who have contributed a wealth of expertise:

Dr. Sherwin Nuland, for his candor in relating his personal experiences with grieving and for his generosity in sharing them: a true "Phoenix Griever."

Peter Moran, Ph.D., colleague and friend, for his cognitive-behavioral wisdom and ongoing enthusiasm for this endeavor.

Dr. Allen Ward, friend and colleague, for his insight into spirituality and adversity.

John Pelletier, Sc.D., friend and colleague, for his insight into the process of forgiveness and for finding the time to support, suggest, and critique.

Robin Casarjian, for so generously sharing her experience and wisdom about forgiveness.

Dean Koontz, for his generous gift of the book *Beautiful Death*, and his gracious permission to use several of his quotes.

Dr. Helen Vassallo, friend and colleague, whose encouragement was there from the beginning.

Nancy Robbins, friend and colleague, whose support and enthusiasm for this project never faltered.

For those whose work eased mine:

Elizabeth Killoran, medical librarian, whose searches uncovered vast reservoirs of information on grief and whose gracious demeanor enhanced the quest.

My dear sister, Jane Wondolowski, whose time spent researching material subtracted from the time I had to.

Ann Steele, who gave her precious time to read and critique the rough drafts.

Jennifer Cummings, who was pressed into action many times and responded genially and efficiently.

A special salute and thanks to my wonderful editor at Jason Aronson, Cindy Hyden. Insightful, incisive, patient, and tactful are descriptors of an ideal editor. She is a role model for all of them. Cindy believed in the message of this book and supported, guided, and nurtured the messenger throughout. Thank you to Jason Aronson, Judy Cohen, and Norma Pomerantz for their expertise, enthusiasm, and encouragement.

My deep and forever thanks to my wonderful family, Al, Alex, and Robyn, who never faltered in their belief and support. I couldn't have asked for better. A special thanks to Adam Marx, my son-in-law, for his valuable contribution to this book. To Al, helpful, supportive, and encouraging in more ways than can ever be measured—with all my love, thank you.

I have had my own teachers in the grief process. Through their deaths, I have experienced what I am writing about. Through their lives, I have been changed. My gratitude and love to my father, baby John, Aunt Connie, Aunt Statia ("Boo"), Kevin, Paula, and Bob.

There is no way to sufficiently thank the Phoenix Grievers. They have given me more than information for a book. They have given me a vision of human potential.

Introduction

You never hear that your life can be better, in a different way, than before the tragedy; that there can be a rainbow after the storm. Or, that something good can be created from such a loss.

Dorothy Labossiere, 1997 (Phoenix Griever)

This is a book about life after the death of a loved one. It is a book about hope. It follows the experiences of the courageous people I call the Phoenix Grievers, named after the mythological bird who, after being consumed in flames, rose from the ashes renewed and in a better form. So it is with these unique human beings. They demonstrate the courage and determination that result in a renaissance of body, mind, and spirit in the aftermath of tragedies.

I am no stranger to the inevitability of death and the impact of loss as the daughter of a doctor and a nurse, in whose clinic I apprenticed from a young age. Over the years, I have personally been affected by grief after the deaths of loved ones. It was my own traditional nursing background that led me to the practice of psychotherapy, specializing for the past twenty-plus years in counseling the bereaved. I have come to recognize a parallel pattern to grief resolution theories to what I had been taught.

When I started working in the bereavement field, grief theories were dominated by messages such as "survive grief," "get through grief," or, "you'll get through it, but you'll never be the same." Such descriptions imply negative or neutral outcomes and do little to encourage grievers to work through the developmental tasks of the process. Only recently are clinicians and theoreticians examining the resiliency of individuals enduring adversity. While indeed a person may not be the same after the death of a loved one, diminishment of self and of life are not the only possible outcomes.

As time went on, I discovered that there are those who can alchemize their pain and despair into something transformative, even inspirational. I came to see that resilience and courage can lead to growth and maturation. And I could not help wondering what makes some grievers surface more empowered than ever, more mature, more compassionate, stronger, while some of the seemingly invulnerable collapse.

None of those I call the Phoenix Grievers has asked for this "opportunity" to evolve. Of course all would gratefully have their loved ones restored to them. Phoenix Grievers do not bypass the grief process. Rather, they experience its phases, accept its challenges, and find ways to create meaning out of loss, thus honoring the life of their deceased. In the words of Jackson (1977), "They met the crisis of their grief in such a way that they grew stronger and more mature because of it" (p. 123).

In this book, we share the subjective experiences of the Phoenix Grievers. We observe and interpret the human potential for growth, meaning, and purpose in life in the aftermath of the loss of a loved one. As we search for role models to guide us in times of emotional and spiritual darkness, we may find them in the Phoenix Grievers. They are the experts.

Specifically, readers will find information and resources regarding:

- understanding our familiarity with grief,
- understanding the five developmental phases of grief,
- using resources and tools to survive and grow through each phase,
- learning what the Phoenix Grievers were like before and after the death of a loved one and how they grew,
- identifying the potential for personal growth during grieving,
- understanding grief's opportunities to create meaning and honor to a loved one's life and death,
- understanding therapeutic metaphor (parable) as a "language" in grief,
- learning a metaphor (parable) for each phase of the grief process.

A parable precedes Chapter 1. It describes, metaphorically, the fear and confusion of grievers beginning their journey through grief. It supports the premise that exceptional grievers can serve as role models for a positive grief outcome and sets the stage for the roles of the Phoenix Grievers presented in this book.

Chapter 1 presents a qualitative description of the attributes of the Phoenix Grievers and links them to traits of exceptional individuals as outlined by authorities such as Maslow (1968), Siebert (1996), Higgins (1994), and Tedeschi and Calhoun (1995).

Chapter 2 introduces the concept of grief as a familiar stranger, a natural life occurrence that we all have experienced many times over the course of our lives. Although the intensity and duration differ, all losses and transitions begin to prepare us for grieving a loved one's death.

A developmental model of the process of grief is formulated from elements of developmental, humanistic, and grief theories. It is called the *Phoenix Model of Grief*, and carries the potential for growth and self-actualization. This chapter provides an understanding of grief, its necessity, its characteristics, and its opportunities through a working model aimed toward a positive outcome.

Chapter 3 describes several Phoenix Grievers' growth through the grief process. Their own words reveal who they were before their losses and who they are now.

Chapters 4 through 8 present the redefined phases and tasks of grief, its anatomy and physiology. Each phase includes a section pertaining to the Phoenix Grievers' recommendations for others based on their experiences. Each phase of grief serves a purpose that is explained. Therapeutic implications conclude each chapter along with recommendations for therapists and the rationale for using particular modalities of treatment during each phase.

Chapter 9 brings us to phase five, Transformation. This new phase describes the growth, maturity, and altruism that are the potential outcomes of grief. It depicts the qualities that the Phoenix Grievers have attained in their long journeys through grief and demonstrate grief's potential for transcendence.

Chapter 10 encapsulates the lessons and "gifts" of the Phoenix Grievers. Their recommendations apply to each phase of grief's journey. Grievers and those who help them will receive wisdom, counsel, and comfort from the teachings of the mentors.

The Epilogue brings the book to a close with a metaphor synopsizing the odyssey of the Phoenix Grievers.

Resources for Therapists and Grievers describes the therapeutic use of metaphor in the grief process. Metaphors are a gentle and subconscious tool for the grievers whose raw wounds may preclude cognitive attention. Several parables for modern-day grievers are included. Each describes a different phase of the grief process.

In order to ensure confidentiality, the Phoenix Grievers chose their own pseudonyms. Public figures gave permission to use their real names. The experiences presented in this book have actually occurred. In order to minimize redundancy, some anecdotes are composites of several similar incidents.

Through this body of work I hope to reach and influence those whose lives have been shattered through the death of a loved one. There is a saying that "there is no other way through it than through it." This is true. However, I believe that there is a distinct path "through it." Those who have been there before can guide and protect others who grieve and facilitate their growth and transformation. Maslow (1968) states that "the study of self-fulfilling people can teach us much about our own mistakes, our shortcomings, the proper directions in which to grow" (p. 5).

The philosophy of this book in no way minimizes the traumatic effects of losing a loved one. What it emphasizes are hope, growth, and transformation through the grieving process, creating meaning from the loss and empowering the mourner. It accentuates grief's potential. Knowing that there is a difference between coping and conquering, the Phoenix Grievers offer the harvest of their experiences.

I believe in the courage and strength of all grievers to overcome adversity. I believe we are all naturally equipped with the right stuff. It is another matter, however, to access the resources and find the courage to use them. The Phoenix Grievers have done exactly that.

As a final note, I would like to add that I hesitated to use adjectives such as exceptional or successful when relating it to grievers because it might imply that there is a correct way to grieve. In reality each person's style is unique. Nevertheless, the grief process contains certain elements that are relatively universal. It is into these common grief responses that the Phoenix Grievers offer their insight and willingly share their experiences of bereavement to empower others who mourn.

I believe it is through spiritual alchemy that we, as mourners, are able to transcend grief and honor our deceased. As a psychotherapist, I am convinced that how we grieve has tremendous potential to enhance our lives so that our loved ones' lives and deaths will not have been in vain.

Now, let us enter the realm of the Phoenix Grievers through an allegorical portal.

Prologue

And it came to pass that the assembly of grievers, knowing that they must pass through the forest of grief, came to the Wise One to seek guidance regarding their forthcoming journey. "It is said, O Wise One, that you know of the perils and hardships of this passage through grief," stated their leader. "We who are about to enter the dark forest wish to prepare ourselves with the tools, skills, and knowledge we need in order to travel safely through the unknown terrain."

"It is so that I hold the map of the territory through which you must pass," replied the Wise One. "I will share my knowledge of the hills and valleys of the area. I will familiarize you with its contours. I will warn you of its pitfalls. Yet, even this will not be enough for you to reach your destination."

The grievers looked at each other with puzzlement. "What more do we need?" their leader asked.

The Wise One reached into the folds of her robe bringing forth several objects that she handed to the grievers. "This cloth is for your tears, that your vision may not be obstructed. This herb is for your pain, that your suffering might not prevent you from continuing your journey. This candle is for light when the darkness is so deep that your path is lost to you. This golden heart is for courage that you may forge onward to your destination."

She then placed the hand of each griever in the hand of the next. "And finally, these hands are for you to hold that you may never be unsupported or alone through this passage."

The Wise One handed a map to each, smiled gently, and counseled, "This may be enough for your journey, but all this is not sufficient for you to reach your destination."

"But Wise One, we have the map, we have guidance and warnings. What more do we need that we might successfully complete our expedition?" questioned their leader.

"It is not enough for you to pass through the forest of grief. For how will you know that you are on the other side and how will you know what you have accomplished and learned from your travels?" challenged the Wise One. "I offer you additional enlightenment so that your mourning may become part of your soul. You need to have faith in your ability to master this journey. You need to have hope that you will grow through the challenges. You need to create meaning from the tragedy of losing one you love. This brings honor to both you and your loved one."

"Yes, this is what we need in order to complete our journey. As soon as you give us these things, we will set forth," stated the chief mourner.

"I cannot give you these gifts," replied the Wise One. "They can only be earned through the journey itself. However, there are those who have gone before you into the forest of grief and have emerged stronger, wiser, and more compassionate than before they began. It is they from whom you must learn."

"Return to the village from whence you came and find those of whom I speak. Listen to their stories, learn from their experiences, and only then may you begin your own pilgrimage," advised the Wise One.

And so it was that the group of grievers went back into their village and sought out the grievers who had gone before them and had returned transformed. From them and from their tales, the grievers learned what they needed to know for their own odyssey. And the transformed grievers offered to serve as guides to the little group, who gratefully accepted. They then set forth into the forest of grief with a new vision and the gift of hope.

1

The Quest

And so it was that the group of grievers returned to the village to search for those of whom the Wise One spoke. From them they hoped to learn how to safely complete their odyssey through grief. . . .

My quest began as a search for answers to these questions:

- Who are the "Phoenix Grievers?"
- How are they different from other grievers?
- Why are they different from other grievers?
- What can other grievers learn from them?

These exceptional individuals look like everyone else. They appear to behave like everyone else, or so it seems, until you know how tragedy has affected their lives. Then, and only then, do you realize how unique they are. They have endured profound personal tragedies and have risen from the ashes of grief as stronger, wiser, and more compassionate human beings. Consider the following:

David, a warm, benevolent, and distinguished gentleman, volunteers in an "Alternatives to Violence" program at a maximum-security prison. His work has helped thousands of prisoners. David's daughter Ruth was raped and murdered.

Noella is a successful psychotherapist, mother, and grandmother, whose helpful hands and loving spirit extend to all in need. Noella's husband Bob died when she was 28 years old, leaving her with two young children and no formal education.

Joyce is a successful research scientist. She is involved with helping bereaved parents, both locally and nationally. Her loving and indomitable spirit is admired by those whose lives she's touched. Years before, Joyce's teen-aged daughter committed suicide, Joyce lost her job, and two years later her husband died, after a stroke and a heart attack, of a "broken heart."

Elizabeth can be counted on to help everyone in need, from family members to friends. She is fully involved in raising her young grandson and active in volunteer services. Seven years ago, Elizabeth's daughter, son-in-law, and granddaughter were killed when a train struck their car. Her grandson was the only survivor.

These individuals are all Phoenix Grievers. Their lives have forever been changed by the deaths of loved ones. They each have a life almost unrecognizable from that which they lived before their tragedies. On meeting them, you might think that life had left them unscathed. You would be very surprised once you heard their stories. You will meet them and others like them in the pages that follow: special people who have grown through the pain and challenges of grieving the death of a loved one.

Phoenix Grievers share the grief symptoms that are common to most of us who have lost a loved one through death. They are not immune to that sorrow. They experience the same depths of pain as others who grieve. Their exceptional outcomes do not mean that their anguish is in any way diminished. The difference is that these people have channeled their pain into something meaningful and constructive. It is their responses to grief and their outcomes that distinguish them from other mourners.

Dr. Al Siebert, renowned authority on the survivor personality (1996), calls them "survivors" and believes that basically they are the same as others. But he also believes that "they survive, cope, and thrive better because they are better at using the inborn abilities possessed by all humans" (p. 1). Clinical psychologist and author Dr. Gina Higgins (1994) says of resilient individuals, "let us consider the resilient not as a unique subspecies, but as fellow travelers, amplifying qualities, dynamics, and potentials inherent in us all" (p. 66). It is both daunting and reassuring to realize that we all have the capacities to transcend life's adversities. Recognizing and accessing these capabilities is one of the greatest challenges in life. In the words of Stephanie, a young woman whose future husband was murdered: "This I know to be true about grief. You are challenged beyond belief at every level and somewhere, somehow, if you really want to, you can transcend it and be a better person and contribute to this world in a better way."

The Phoenix Grievers choose to live fully and to help others from the abundance of their bounty. As you read about their personal experiences with grieving, you will see many demonstrations of the human propensity for courage in the face of adversity and growth in the aftermath of grief. As Siebert (1996), wrote: "Your past experiences will always be a part of you. You can't eradicate them, but even the most horrible experiences can be dealt with so they do not ruin your life. It is possible, also, that by working to overcome your emotional trauma, you go beyond recovery. You may develop a better, stronger version of yourself than you suspected could exist" (p. 238). As did the Phoenix Grievers.

> "You may develop a better, stronger version of yourself than you suspected could exist."
>
> —Siebert

In general, Phoenix Grievers have

- experienced the death of one or more loved ones

- accepted and mastered the challenges of grief
- demonstrated growth and transformation through grief
- created meaning from the loved one's life and death
- inspired and helped others through adversity.

In other words, Phoenix Grievers do not just emerge on the other side of grief the same as when they entered. They grow, mature, develop new strengths, and continue developing their unique potential. They continue to recognize themselves as who they were but are astonished at who they have become. Life's experiences have been woven into the fabric of their souls. As you read their inspirational stories the process of their transformative experiences becomes indisputable. The characteristics of the Phoenix Grievers show themselves again and again. They

- are more self-tolerant and tolerant of others
- are more flexible
- have a deeper sense of humor
- have developed some creativity
- take more risks (having a child, going to school, learning a new skill, and helping others)
- have a more positive outlook in the face of trouble; they believe in their ability to handle it.
- do not accept a victim role in life
- more lovingly place their families first
- are more compassionate toward others
- have spiritual alchemy: the ability to convert something negative into something positive
- have created meaning out of their loved one's life and death
- have a deeper spirituality; trust in a higher force and a purpose in life
- appreciate their growth and transcendence.

What I found interesting about this list is that many of these characteristics are similar to those described by humanistic psychologist Abraham Maslow (1968) in his identification of the self-actualized person and by clinical psychologist Al Siebert (1996) in his definition of the survivor personality. Both single out such personality traits as curiosity, a nonjudgmental attitude, the ability to laugh at oneself, empathy, a positive outlook in the face of tribulation, and the capacity to convert misfortune into a gift and make full use of innate potential.

Siebert (1996) believes that "people seldom tap into their deepest strengths and abilities until forced to do so by a major adversity" (p. 7). It appears that the very process of going through bereavement presents an opportunity to develop skills, strengths, and wisdom. This would suggest that tragedy can force growth and lead to self-actualization more rapidly than a normal developmental time frame. It would also appear that this growth takes place through a revolutionary rather than an evolutionary process.

One significant quality is the ability to create a positive meaning from a negative experience: what I refer to as *spiritual alchemy*. An alchemist is a person who has the power to change or transmute something into another form or state of being, as in the ancient legends of turning lead into gold. Phoenix Grievers are such alchemists. They channel their grief into something meaningful and constructive.

As they moved into grief, the Phoenix Grievers were forced to confront and change some of their fundamental beliefs about themselves and life. In the process of redefining themselves, they needed to disconnect from the expectations of others. Their perceptions, beliefs, attitudes, and behaviors began to reflect a new doctrine of self. Without these changes, their growth would have been impossible because the old beliefs would not support the vision that something good could come out of the tragedy of losing a loved one.

Phoenix Grievers evidence growth in four areas: self, relationships, beliefs, and spirituality. The most dramatic and pivotal change takes place within the self. Because our thoughts, feelings, and actions follow what the self perceives, it is easy to see the profound implications of these changes. One young widow reflected, "For a long while after he died, I perceived myself to be powerless to cope with life. I had no confidence in myself, so I didn't bother trying." In contrast, another widow affirmed, "There was just no option for me. I firmly believed in my ability to survive, build a life for myself, the best life possible." The latter, one of our Phoenix Grievers, echoes many when she says, "I refuse to be a victim." What each perceived to be true about herself determined her ability to go forward after losing a spouse. Beliefs about the self are critical in determining whether a griever merely survives grief or surpasses it.

This perceptual shift also influences a mourner's attitude and behavior toward others. Phoenix Grievers value their loved ones more and, interestingly, suffer fools less. They are reluctant to spend a lot of time with negative or draining people. Most are intolerant of people who whine or refuse to help themselves. They save their precious time and energy to spend on their families and on satisfying friendships and interests. If they devote time to help needy others, they choose to do so in order to help relieve suffering and deprivation.

Phoenix Grievers report changed beliefs about their purposes in life and life in general. They feel empowered to fulfill their purposes and are committed to making a difference in others' lives. As an extension of that belief they create meaning from their loved ones' lives and deaths. A young woman whose mother died says, "It's up to me to create meaning from her death and from what I learned from her in her lifetime. I will live in a way to make her proud."

Phoenix Grievers frequently use the descriptor "compassionate" when talking about how they have changed. They describe their feelings of sharing, understanding, and wanting to help another person who is suffering. They "blend" with the other's experience in a way that does not bring harm to themselves. As one bereaved mother put it, "I can put myself in someone else's shoes now and understand how they must feel. This makes me more sensitive to the different ways people cope and I am less judgmental when that behavior is different from mine."

Paradoxically, the Phoenix Grievers discuss their struggle with what they call "negative outcomes." One is in the area of tolerance and the other is in allowing themselves to love again, both contexts in which they also report growth. One grieving father expresses the sentiment of many Phoenix Grievers: "I had no tolerance for whiners. After losing my child, their petty complaints annoyed me because they have nothing to snivel about. I am working on this intolerance but I'm not totally free of it." A young widow says, "I was more aware of the risk of loving again and I became cautious and wary in relating to new people. As time went on, I found the courage to face the fears and I let myself love again."

Phoenix Grievers readily admit to what they feel are negative personality characteristics. They are aware, they are accountable, and they work on change. In other words, they take action. One grieving mother admits, "I've gone backward in my work on anger over the years of grieving. I used to be able to control my volatile temper, but I've regressed. However, I am working on that control again and I see a little progress." Phoenix Grievers do not stop growing.

Most Phoenix Grievers have come to terms with their inner spirituality. They make the distinction between religion (someone else's beliefs coming from the outside) and spirituality (self-generated beliefs coming from the inside). There is often a blending of both. Most believe in a higher power although they may lack words to describe this concept. Others are content to build their spirituality as they move on in life. "I'm not too sure about God, but that's okay for now," says one griever. Whatever their germinating truth is about God, Phoenix Grievers have exceptional appreciation and respect for their own life and the lives of others, human or not, and a positive outlook about their own places and purposes in life.

Most Phoenix Grievers are unaware of the transformation taking place while they are going through the grieving process. However, in retrospect, the phenomenon becomes apparent. It would appear that although death came as a situational crisis, their growth and achievement contained elements of a developmental process. This developmental prototype forms the structure of the Phoenix Model and will be described in Chapter 2.

The Phoenix Grievers can serve as role models, living prophecies of grief's potential. Dr. Sherwin Nuland (personal communication 1997), renowned author and surgeon, relates his observations on role models after the death of his mother when he was 11 years old. "I developed a reliance on a 'firmament of stars' outside of the family for my models of the way American achievements are created."

The exceptional women and men you will meet in this book are a "firmament of stars" for those who have lost a loved one and for those who are committed to guiding and comforting others through grief. Let us begin the discovery of how they accomplished their transformation. To do that, we must understand what the journey entails and why it is necessary.

And so the mourners began their search for those of wisdom and growth who had been transformed by their journeys through grief. . . .

2

Anatomy and Physiology of Grief

And so they set forth on their quest, but they knew not why. . . .

THE FAMILIAR STRANGER

It may surprise you to learn that we are all experienced grievers. Whether or not you've ever lost a loved one to death, you *have* experienced some sort of loss. The losses can be so small, so subtle, that we do not define our reaction to them as grief. Perhaps you've called it the "blahs," the blues, or just a bad mood. I use the term *mini-grief* to describe our reaction to life's smaller losses. Loss and the grief that follows come in all shapes and sizes as you will see from the following examples.

Situational loss occurs when we are deprived of a valued person, pet, belonging, or tangible item. Grief may have more serious consequences after events such as prolonged unemployment, health impairment, depression, or the end of a marriage. Even occurrences that may appear less than tragic— the final failure of a trusted old car or flunking a test—can be significant enough to trigger a mini-grief. We mourn what we have lost.

Developmental loss and the subsequent grief can be thought of as growing pains, grief as a result of transition from one stage of development to the next. The very act of being born involves separation, a loss of sorts. As we move through each stage of life, from childhood to puberty, from adulthood into senior citizenship, we leave some parts of ourselves behind and take on new roles and challenges. Life's movement creates loss and, therefore, we grieve. Over and over, we experience the cycle of letting go of the old and adapting to the new. Every rotation through the cycle means a brush with grief on some level. Change and letting go are ingredients of life as well as ingredients of grief.

Existential loss or disillusionment might seem relatively easy to dismiss. However, losing one's hope, beliefs, or assumptions about the world can be almost as traumatic as losing a loved one. Consider the pain and subsequent grief of learning that a friend has betrayed you, or the despair of realizing that a long-held dream will never come true. It can seem as if the world has suddenly shifted underneath you. The grief caused by existential loss can be profound.

As if our personal experiences were not enough, stories from the media or from friends can inspire "second-hand" feelings of grief. We may feel melancholy and preoccupied after hearing of a particularly poignant tragedy, whether or not we know the people involved. Our hearts go out in sympathy to the families of victims of violence and accidents. We feel an inkling of the grief that we might have felt if it had been one of our own loved ones.

The loss of public figures can cause grief as well. The assassinations of John F. Kennedy and Martin Luther King and, more recently, the back-to-back deaths of Princess Diana and Mother Theresa, provoked both mourning and deep existential loss—the so-called loss of innocence. However distant celebrities might be, we grieve personally the loss of their presence and all that they represented to us.

In ways large and small, intimate and distant, grief continually touches our lives. Why is it, then, that so many consider themselves ill prepared to handle grief following the loss of someone close? Situational, developmental, existential, and second-hand losses can all be seen as preparatory events, a training of sorts, for the major life crises. Mini-griefs familiarize us with the consequences of loss.

We do not have to enter grief's door as novices. Each of us has experienced tears, guilt, fatigue, sadness, disbelief, irritability, anger, fear—all the components of grief—without necessarily labeling them as such. We already possess the resources we need to cope with grief. With some information, guidance, and reassurance, we can apply these skills and learn to live without a loved one, heal our wounds, and begin to build a different life.

Awareness and information are fundamental tools for working through grief. Psychoeducation can be a useful tool. Mark, a Phoenix Griever whose daughter died, said, "Grief and death are not normal dinner conversations. They are avoided so you don't get the emotional exposure before death happens." Understanding the dynamics of grief helps to clarify the process grievers are undergoing. This knowledge and guidance can empower them, bringing them one step closer toward healing.

WHAT IS GRIEF?

The death of a loved one changes the normal flow and rhythm of life, forever dividing it into *before* and *after*. Grief is the means by which we cope with that division. It serves as the transition point between two continuums of living: the life of before, with the loved one, and the

> The death of a loved one changes the normal flow and rhythm of life, forever dividing it into *before* and *after*.

life after, without. Grief is a passage from yesterday to tomorrow, an area where challenges and opportunities coexist. Therein lies the *potential* of grief. It functions as a bridge to the future.

Grief is a process that is activated when loss occurs. It is the natural, elemental response to losing someone to whom we are attached. Responses to loss have even been observed among animals as diverse as elephants, chimpanzees, geese, and dogs (Bowlby 1961).

Grief is so much more than sadness. It is complex and multidimensional. It is "a response to bereavement; it is how the survivor feels. It is also how the survivor thinks, eats, sleeps and makes it through the day" (Kastenbaum 1986, p. 136). It can and does influence the mind, body, and spirit. It can be brief or lengthy. It can obstruct our daily lives or leave no visible impression. It can bring out the best or the worst in us. It can render us greater or lesser human beings.

> Grief is . . . "how the survivor thinks, eats, sleeps and makes it through the day."
>
> —Kastenbaum

Psychologist Dr. Therese A. Rando (1988), distinguished authority on death and grief, explains: "Grief reaches into every part of your life, touching your work, your relationship with others and your image of yourself" (p. 25). Grief can temporarily disrupt or permanently alter your thoughts and beliefs, emotions, behavior—even the anatomy and physiology of the body. When stunned by grief, any and all normal human functions are subject to change.

Barbara, a 43-year-old widow relates her experience after her husband died of a sudden heart attack. "I truly thought I was going crazy. I had always prided myself on my calm, logical approach to life. My friends used to call me laid back, but now I was a basket case. I couldn't control anything inside of me. I felt like I was going to pieces."

She remembers being "startled by the rush of painful emotions," while staring at her husband's favorite snacks in the supermarket. "I wasn't prepared for the impact of these feelings and I just about made it out of the store before I lost it."

The "crazy" feelings that Barbara describes are actually a *sane* response to grief. Reflect on the following examples— all symptoms of normal grief:

- distorted thinking patterns, "crazy" and/or irrational thoughts, fearful thoughts
- feelings of despair and hopelessness
- out of control or numbed emotions
- changes in sensory perceptions (sight, taste, smell, etc.)
- memory lags and mental "short-circuits"
- inability to concentrate
- obsessive focus on the loved one
- losing track of time
- increase or decrease of appetite and/or sexual desire
- difficulty falling or staying asleep
- dreams in which the deceased seems to visit the griever
- nightmares in which death themes are repeated
- physical illnesses like the flu, headaches, or other maladies
- symptoms that mimic the disease that killed the loved one
- shattered beliefs about life, the world, and even God

Considering this staggering array of symptoms, it's easy to understand why some theorists, including Engel (1961), considered grief to be an illness from which the griever needs to recover. More recently, though, we have begun to look at grief in a new way. We have learned much about the resilience of people in grief by looking beyond the symptoms of pain to the underlying reasons we grieve.

Why Do We Grieve?

The short answer to this question is "because we love." Every individual who risks loving another is vulnerable to the threat of loss and thus at risk for experiencing grief. Love, this marvel that brings the greatest of pleasure, carries the potential for the greatest of pain. "The pain of grief is just as much a part of life as the joy of love. It is perhaps the price we pay for love, the cost of commitment" (Parkes 1972, pp. 5–6). What cruel irony! There are those who would ask, "Is loving someone worth it?" The voices of the Phoenix Grievers echo the response of Michelle, a bereaved mother.

"After Marie died, I was going to pray for no more pain in life; then I realized that with love comes pain. I guess I'd rather love and risk the hurt and loss than not love at all. That would not be living."

To understand grief, therefore, we must look at the nature of love. Loving someone is an act that affects mind, body, emotions, and soul. The smell, taste, touch, sound, and feel of the loved one permeate our senses and we respond at a deep level. It seems as if we can actually feel the imprint of our loved ones in our bodies and minds. The sensations of holding our loved one within us are easy to recognize but difficult to define. "When I love someone, I just know how it feels inside," says one mourner. Since love is experienced in so many ways, we feel the loss on many levels. The void caused by the death of a loved one is directly correlated to the depth of our attachment.

Michelle, the grieving mother, "felt the ripping of the bonds of attachment to my child as physically as if they were torn from my physical body. There were times when I doubled over from the pain."

To love another requires an investment of time, emotion, and energy. When someone we love dies, that precious investment of self is wiped out. Grieving presents opportunities to rebuild this emotional capital. The same qualities that allowed us to create and invest in a portfolio of love remain within us. Those qualities are part of who we are. Nuland (1997) explains that grief is a kind of proof "that one is capable of . . . love. That one has felt in a particular way about someone one has lost and the knowledge of being able to feel that way is strengthening in itself. This is a very reassuring thing when we look at who we are. I am more of a man because I . . . have loved certain people I have now lost."

When we love someone, we also come to love the parts of ourselves that blossom in the relationship. This deepens our love for whoever has brought out the best in us. Initially, it may appear that these parts have been lost along with the loved one.

> When we love someone, we also come to love the parts of ourselves that blossom in the relationship.

Gary's wife Kim was killed in an automobile accident. He remembers what she brought out in him. "I never realized how caring and unselfish I could be; and, yes, romantic. My devotion to her and then, our baby, was so all encompassing. It felt good. Sure, we had our rough times, but I believed in us and our life together. I liked me!"

We may attribute these new parts of ourselves to the loved one, thinking he or she gave them to us. When that person dies, we may erroneously believe that our new qualities also die. Yet it is important to remember that we, ourselves, have brought forth these virtues. Take, for example, a mother who has lost a child. The loss does not change her ability to be a good mother. She maintains her qualities of nurturing, unconditional loving, and unselfishness, even though the child is no longer there. All of the qualities we have, both positive and negative, are resources to help us in our lives. We need to learn how to use them constructively.

So far, we have seen that grief is an affirmation that we have loved. Let us ask once again, "Why do we grieve?" The death of a loved one introduces a crisis into normal life, disrupting the here-and-now state of being. When normal life turns to chaos, disaster feels imminent. However, once freed from habits and routines, growth can emerge from the very same chaos that threatens ruin. Interestingly, the Chinese symbol for crisis is a combination of the characters for "danger" and "opportunity." A crisis contains the potential to improve the body, mind, and spirit.

Since all loss involves change and all change requires adaptation, adaptation can be seen as one of the keys to growth and survival. In fact, the *American Heritage Dictionary* (1979) defines adaptation as "an alteration or adjustment in structure or habits . . . by which a species or individual improves its condition in relationship to its environment" (p. 14). Note that the word *improves* is part of this definition. The death of a loved one can be viewed as a catalyst for positive change.

However, before growth can occur, the chaos must be calmed. The calm comes only when we submit to the chaos. Like the oft-cited willow tree that bends in the storm but does not break, it is those who bend and adapt to grief's force who survive and even transcend the crisis. In many ways grief *is* a process of adaptation, nature's response to change. Grief is necessary to heal and grow after someone we love dies. It allows us to integrate the old and new together to form a new life. It moves us from the past, through the present, and toward a future without that precious person. Life experiences over the years have taught me that people have incredible strengths that enable them to transcend tragedy. We must begin by understanding that we each possess the resources to adapt to both the good and bad that life brings, and also that growth and transformation are potential outcomes of grief.

One's perception of grief is a key factor in its outcome. Beliefs often lead to self-fulfilling prophecies. If grievers believe the process of grief can only have a negative outcome they may be disheartened rather than helped. On the other hand, the belief that grief can lead to a positive outcome may give the griever enough courage to begin the journey. The knowledge that strength and growth can be gained by fully experiencing grief can encourage a bereaved person. It gives purpose and meaning to the pain. Suffering should not be in vain. Grief holds the potential for growth and transformation. This concept is one of the most compelling reasons for the writing of this book.

HOW DO WE GRIEVE?

So far, we have learned that grief is a response to loss marking the division of before and after. The bridge between before and after can also be a road to opportunity. Grief work explains how we are to cross that bridge. Lindemann (1944), in his classic study of grief, coined the term *grief work* to describe the process that takes place between one's initial reaction and eventual adaptation to the death of a loved one. After hearing a description of the tasks to be accomplished during grief work, a grieving widow said: "It sounds like a job description and I don't want the job." Unfortunately, this formidable work must be accomplished when mourners have the least amount of strength.

Authorities on grief (Rando 1988, Worden 1991) agree that certain tasks need to be accomplished in order to proceed through the grieving process toward a healthy resolution. In other words, you don't just sit and wait for time to "fix it." Passively waiting for healing is contraindicated in grieving. Mourners need to work on grief rather than have grief work on

> Mourners need to work on grief rather than have grief work on them.

them. The strategic factor is *how* one deals with the tasks of grief.

Although there are predictable and universal aspects of grieving, each person's experience is unique. The phases and their tasks are most often described in chronological sequence, but in reality, they assume a "hopscotch" sequence: individuals may proceed through two or three phases only to find themselves back to "start" some six months later. One widower recalled, "I thought I had graduated from phases two and three, so when I felt the waves of grief crash over me, it took me by surprise. I was disappointed and frustrated."

Often the death of another loved one will revive grief feelings previously experienced. I call such setbacks *grief revisited.* They are usually temporary. When mourners choose the opportunities that grieving offers, former growths will be regained and additional strengths and resources attained. The completion of the tasks in each phase opens the door to the next sequence. Understanding grief and taking the steps to work within its parameters reassures the bereaved and empowers them to complete their grief work.

Re-experiencing previously completed grief work occurs at both predictable and unpredictable times. Anniversaries, birthdays, weddings, and times of developmental transition such as puberty, menopause, becoming a parent, even the "empty nest" passage will regenerate grief. Other unpredictable stimuli might be music, smells, sounds, or images that bring the lost loved one to mind and heart. This back-and-forth movement between the phases of grief is natural and should be anticipated.

Some grievers may experience several phases almost simultaneously. For instance, a grieving person who is also the family provider may have to return to work immediately and must adapt to life without the loved one while experiencing symptoms of shock, anger, profound sorrow, depression, and all else that follows. For others, the phases overlap and may be re-experienced later on in the grief cycle or many years afterward. This is the *rhythm* of grief.

Ultimately, mourners' choices determine healthy or unhealthy adaptive steps toward the future. Consider two children killed in a hit-and-run accident, two grieving mothers, two individual responses to grief. One of the mothers began to drink and didn't stop until she was no longer physically or mentally healthy; thus two losses were created from one tragedy. The other mother became depressed, sought treatment, and, once recovered, began to rebuild and expand her life. She volunteered as a facilitator in a self-help organization for bereaved parents. She created gains from her tragedy. As you will see, the grieving process can be a formula of addition, subtraction, or multiplication. It is how grievers accommodate that holds the potential for regression, stagnation, or growth.

A DEVELOPMENTAL MODEL OF GROWTH

During more than twenty years of practice, I've come to notice the striking similarity between grievers who thrive in the aftermath of loss and the self-actualized personality described by Maslow. He identified "people who have developed or are developing to the full stature of which they are capable" (1987, p. 126). This self-actualized personality sits at the top of a hypothetical pyramid called "The Hierarchy of Needs" (see Figure 2–1). This hierarchy reflects Maslow's theory that humans are inherently motivated by needs and that those needs must be met in a particular order. In other words, our higher needs cannot be filled until the lower ones are satisfied. Growth occurs through meeting the needs of each level.

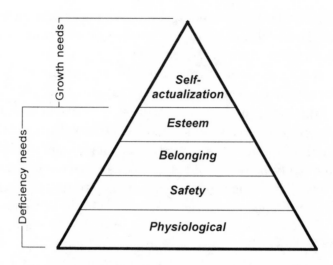

Figure 2–1. Maslow's Hierarchy of Needs

At the base of Maslow's pyramid are the fundamental, *physiological* needs for food, water, oxygen, rest, and sleep. Until these needs are met, no further growth can occur. Once the primary needs are satisfied, the *safety* needs arise; we seek security, stability, protection, and freedom from fear and anxiety. The *belonging* needs for love, affection, and connection to others follow. Work, home, school, religious organizations and other circles of society are sources for the belonging needs. Beyond these are the *esteem needs*: needs to be competent, adequate, useful, and necessary in the world, contributing to a positive regard for oneself and the respect of others.

The physiological, safety, belonging, and esteem needs can be grouped together as the "deficiency" needs. The ability to fulfill them is dependent on forces outside the individual. One cannot survive if there is no food or water, one cannot sleep if there is no physiological or physical safety, nor can one belong if one is shunned or if one feels alienated or isolated. One cannot feel safe without protection, or competent without the opportunity to try. When the deficiency needs have been sufficiently and reasonably (if not completely) met, the individual feels somewhat full and stable. There is the confidence that comes with mastery over challenges and the feeling of being appreciated and valued by others. We would describe such a person as healthy and well-adjusted. Yet, according to Maslow, some of us are inspired to be more than just well-adjusted.

Some are driven to fulfill their unique potential (1970), symbolized at the very top of the hierarchy as the need for *self-actualization*. Unlike the deficiency needs, the desire for growth arises from an inner desire to express oneself. This movement toward growth usually takes place on a subconscious level; the individual is not necessarily even aware of striving toward self-actualization (1970).

A DEVELOPMENTAL MODEL OF GRIEF

The Phoenix Model expands on Maslow's theory by integrating it with a specific life crisis: the death of a loved one and its ensuing grief. Based on my own and others' research and observations, I have defined five phases of grief that correlate strongly with Maslow's hierarchy of needs. It is through meeting these needs that the tasks of grief are successfully accomplished and growth is achieved. While others have written about the stages of grief, the Phoenix Model differs in that it is a developmental prototype rather than a crisis model. Although grief occurs after a situational crisis (death of a loved one), the passage through it has developmental components. As with all passages in life, grief contains its own predictable sequence and tasks. Therefore, the passage through grief may be conceptualized as a *developmental* process. This developmental perspective offers a unique approach to understanding the process. It provides a guide for grievers, therapists, and supportive others. This paradigm becomes further developed as we follow the Phoenix Grievers' experiences.

Unlike Maslow's subjects, who did not reach self-actualization before the age of 60, if at all (Petri 1981), the Phoenix Grievers achieved growth rapidly, many at a very young age. How is it then, that the Phoenix Grievers of this book reached the peak of the hierarchy? The answers lie in how they worked through each level from the base to the apex of the developmental hierarchy. It is my belief that these exceptional grievers reached self-actualization through *revolution* (crisis-induced) rather than *evolution* (normally paced development). Phoenix Grievers faced the challenges of forced growth under a very difficult circumstance: the death of a loved one.

Maslow (1970) addressed the impact of crisis on his theory of growth and motivation. He believed that even healthy individuals would regress to a deprivation need level when emotionally or physically threatened with danger. In the case of grief, danger comes in the form of a crisis—the death of a loved one. Regardless of how far one has developed along the hierarchy of needs, the death of a loved one sends one down to the very bottom of the pyramid.

Since Phoenix Grievers ultimately make their way to the top of the pyramid, although grief plunges them first to the bottom, it would follow that they pass through each level of Maslow's hierarchy on their way. It's as if the momentum they gain during the ascent propels them further up than they were before.

The Phoenix Model organizes grief into five phases that closely parallel the phases in Maslow's model of the development of a self-actualized person. Each stage of grief as described by the Phoenix Model represents a movement up the hierarchy; by working through the phases of grief, one is, simultaneously, working up the hierarchy of needs. The phases are *Impact, Chaos, Adaptation, Equilibrium,* and *Transformation.* The first four incorporate those in existing literature and you may recognize them by the terms shock, denial, disorganization, and reorganization. I have renamed and further defined the phases of grief and have added a fifth to account for the Phoenix phenomenon. This new paradigm describes the growth that can take place during and beyond grief.

The addition of a fifth stage, Transformation, contains the message of this book—a positive outcome from grief. Transformation goes beyond what you may currently understand to be part of grief. It expands on Maslow's definition of self-actualization and incorporates aspects of the synergistic personality as advanced by Siebert (1996). This personality type makes the world a better place for others and, thereby, for himself. He is ethical, proactive in anticipating trouble, and generally content with his life. The experiences of the Phoenix Grievers demonstrate and support the existence of this phase. The integration of the needs and tasks of Maslow's hierarchy of needs and the Phoenix phases of grief provide a sequence of tasks toward growth and transformation (see Table 2–1).

Table 2–1. Integrating Maslow's Hierarchy of Needs into the Phoenix Model of Grief

Maslow's Hierarchy of Needs		Phoenix Model of Grief	
At this stage,	individuals seek to fill these needs:	At this stage,	grievers are:
Physiological	nourishment, shelter, rest, sleep	*Impact*	processing the reality of the death while sustaining physiological needs
Safety/Security	stability, familiarity, predictability, freedom from fear and anxiety	*Chaos*	developing order and structure from chaos, expressing emotions of grief

Maslow's Hierarchy of Needs		Phoenix Model of Grief	
Belonging	connecting to others, feeling understood, feeling accepted, giving and receiving love and affection	*Adaptation*	adapting to life without the loved one, seeking connection to others through support systems, other grievers, work, school, house of worship, renewing hope, taking risks, developing new roles
Self-esteem	developing competencies, finding appreciation and respect from self and others	*Equilibrium*	maintaining growth, choosing (new) direction in life, attaining stability and balance in life, considering developing self-potential
Self-actualization	developing self-potential	*Transformation*	developing self-potential, greater spirituality, altruism, self-awareness, acceptance of self and others, appreciation for life.

The death of a loved one precipitates the syndrome of grief beginning with the first phase, *Impact*. The news of the death throws the griever out of balance, causing even the most stable of individuals to plummet to a base level of functioning. The griever's very physiological equilibrium is threatened.

Shock, denial, and disbelief quickly give way to anxiety, fear, and confusion as the griever affirms the reality of death, which recognition marks the entrance to *Chaos*, phase two of the Phoenix Model. Most especially compromised are the safety and security elements of the griever's life. The first two phases of the Phoenix Model, Impact and Chaos, closely parallel the first two levels of Maslow's hierarchy of needs. Grievers need to stabilize their physiological and psychological needs as they struggle to come out of shock and the devastation to their safety and security modes of being. They must reasonably satisfy these needs before advancing to the next set.

During the third phase, *Adaptation*, the griever must continue to meet the needs of the previous two phases while attempting to adjust to the new environment without the loved one. This requires risk taking and the development and mastery of new roles. Adaptation represents the most active of all the phases. During this phase, the lower needs (physiological, safety) on Maslow's hierarchy are met and the issues raised by Impact and Chaos are being resolved.

The belonging needs of the Adaptation phase are starting to be met as the griever begins reaching out to others for support and guidance. By successfully addressing these needs, the griever also begins to develop a sense of self-esteem that heralds the onset of the fourth phase, *Equilibrium*.

Spanning the end of the Adaptation phase and the beginning of the Equilibrium phase, the griever needs to stabilize and obtain mastery over the environment through developing new skills and competencies. These compensate for those lost to the relationship by the death of the loved one and those required for successful functioning in the new life. Through further empowerment over the environment the griever is beginning to meet the needs of the next level, which are those of self-esteem.

The griever is attaining some mastery and feels useful in a new way. Simultaneously, the griever is receiving encouragement and recognition from others, and now risks new behaviors, tolerates frustration, and continues to maintain the gains of the former levels of growth. At the end of this fourth phase, Equilibrium, mourners' lives are stable, gratifying, familiar, and fulfilling. For most people, this is adequate.

For the Phoenix Grievers, this is not enough. They are the minority who continue to pursue an advanced level of life participation, what Maslow called self-actualization and what I call *Transformation*. Only when Equilibrium is attained is there the choice to develop the potential that lies within each of us. Since the decision to continue growing is a choice, it is fair to say that Transformation is optional. For those who choose to accept the challenge of the fifth phase, the rewards cannot be disputed. See Table 2–2.

Table 2–2. The Phoenix Model of Grief for Therapists

Phase	Needs For:	Challenges To:	Intervention Use:
Impact	Physiological stability, safety, security	Break down denial	Crisis intervention in a humanistic manner
	Protection from anxiety and fear	Acknowledge death of loved one	More directive approach
			Establish support team
Chaos	Safety, security, attachment, and belonging	Feel and express pain of grief, safely, healthily	Continue crisis intervention with more directive approach toward solution-oriented therapy and establishing support team
	Structure and order	Stay connected to and supported by others	Connect to others

Phase	Needs For:	Challenges To:	Intervention Use:
Adaptation	Belonging, risk taking, with new roles	Be in the world without the loved one	Humanistic, solution-oriented and/or cognitive-behavioral therapies
	Beginning self-confidence and self-esteem	Maintain previous growth.	
		Develop new roles	
Equilibrium	Belonging, self-esteem, self-confidence	Integrate new skills and qualities	Humanistic and supportive
		Maintain balance in new life	Cognitive-behavioral if beliefs impede growth
		Develop spirituality	
Transformation	Self-actualization	Fulfilling unique self-potential	Humanistic and supportive
		Discovering purpose	
		Creating meaning	
		Altruism	

Should "grief revisited" occur, intervention should cycle back to Impact or Chaos, depending on assessment.

SUMMARY

- Grief is a "familiar stranger" that is activated when situational, developmental, and/or existential losses occur.
- Grief is not a passive state. It involves accomplishing certain tasks.
- The Phoenix Model of Grief resembles Maslow's developmental pyramid in that it presupposes the opportunity for self-actualization.
- Each phase of grief contains needs and challenges that, when successfully met, move grievers to a higher level of development and maturity.
- The Phoenix model of grief consists of five phases. They are Impact, Chaos, Adaptation, Equilibrium, and Transformation.
- The Phoenix Model of Grief offers a new approach toward understanding grief as a natural, developmental transition of life leading to a positive outcome.

The little group continued their pursuit of those who had gone before them into grief's journey....

3

The Discovery

And the grievers searched far and wide for those of whom the Wise One spoke, but they found no one who appeared any different from themselves. And they were bewildered . . . .

BEFORE AND AFTER

You would like a Phoenix Griever if you met one. They are warm, open, and approachable human beings with whom other people feel comfortable. You might think how self-confident, centered, and together they are, how lucky they are. When you discovered more about their stories, you might then feel incredulity followed by admiration. These people have experienced the best and the very worst that life has to offer. You will read some of their stories in this chapter.

Their chronicles are separated into two sections: bereavement through natural causes and bereavement through catastrophic causes. The first section focuses on natural causes, referring to deaths caused by a disease process or failure of the internal anatomy or physiology necessary to sustain life. The natural causes in this section do not include cases of sudden death.

Many of the individuals bereaved through natural causes may have had some time to adapt to the inevitability of death. They may have already assumed new roles and adjusted to unfamiliar responsibilities while also focusing energy, time, and attention on caring for the loved one. The neglected needs of the caregiver may lead to personal exhaustion and burnout. When multiple stresses coexist, as with lengthy dying trajectories, the caregiver is placed in a suspended state. The caregiver may suffer from ambivalence and an overlay of guilt, anger, and confusion, which combine to create their own challenges.

The second section, bereavement through catastrophic causes, refers to deaths precipitated externally. They are usually sudden and sometimes multiple. The unanticipated crisis catches the individual off-guard. There is no time to prepare. Initially, coping is more difficult and the elements of shock, disbelief, and denial are more apt to trigger an emotional or physical collapse. The griever's resources and strengths may not be readily available or sufficiently developed. The griever needs time to respond to the demands of the crisis, particularly in acknowledging that a death has occurred and in assuming new roles.

The personal narratives of the Phoenix Grievers describe their experiences with the loss of a loved one and compare what they were like before and what they are like now.

PART ONE: BEREAVEMENT THROUGH NATURAL CAUSES

Death of a Spouse

Noella was 28 years old when her husband Bob suffered a severe stroke. She was catapulted into a caregiving, breadwinning, single-parent role for which she was woefully unprepared.

She says, "I lacked maturity and self-confidence. I was totally defined by others' expectations of me: *his* wife, *their* mother, *their* sister, *her* daughter. Who was I?

"The changes in me have been dramatic. I was forced to grow. My new abilities to care for Bob and my family infused confidence in my adaptive and survival skills. My capacities for patience, tolerance, and compassion increased and continued to reflect my growing self-image.

"After Bob died, I began to make decisions for our futures; my self-confidence was emerging. I returned to school to become a teacher and, later, a psychotherapist, so I could share what I had learned and earned in order to help others through crises. I was determined not only to survive, but to thrive. I refused to say, 'why me?' I refused to be a victim.

"Today, I am very content with my life. I have wonderful children, a career, new creativity, and financial stability. There is balance and harmony in my world. I am grateful for everything in life and proud of who I am."

Noella's growth is evident. She is now self-defined with a high self-esteem earned through meeting the challenges of Bob's illness and death and the new roles she has had to assume. The joyful spirit she was born with, combined with a forced maturity, produced a very loving and competent woman. The patience, tolerance, and compassion she developed through the long years of caregiving made psychotherapy a natural career choice. Noella is making a difference in peoples' lives and thus she has created meaning from the tragedy of Bob's death.

Death of a Young Daughter

The joyous birth of twins, a boy, Derek, and a girl, Marie, after a miscarriage and a stillbirth, fulfilled the promise of Michelle's dream of having a family and restored her trust in God. When Marie was three, she died of cancer of the liver. For Michelle, it was a trust betrayed, a dream turned nightmare. She recalls:

"It's hard to remember the me of eleven years ago and because I'm always changing and growing, my description of my present self will be outdated in no time.

"What I was like before, and now after, is like comparing a block of concrete to a featherbed. Not only did I expect myself to be perfect, I expected others to behave according to my view of the world. I had perfect grades, was never late, my home was spotless, even meals were made from scratch.

"You can only imagine what Marie's death did to my view of life. Nothing was real or familiar anymore. I had become an alien in my own world, both internally and externally.

"Looking back, this is what I see and looking in the mirror of the present I see my Self. I no longer need anyone's approval to feel good about myself. Somewhere along the way I've become competent. I've had to learn to cope with what life really gives us—unpredictability. If I can do that, I can do anything. I took many risks, but having another child five years after Marie died was the most frightening of all.

"Ann is wonderful and has passed the age that Marie died and I can breathe a little sigh of relief. I have volunteered for several years now, soup kitchens and Parents Anonymous, wanting to give back some of fullness of who I am to others.

"My old standard of perfection is reflected in the new way I have accommodated my home to my family, not the other way around. We live *in* the house, not *for* the house. Sometimes I go all out and bake from scratch, but now I let my reality determine what I can accomplish.

"I have the courage and compassion to be present for those in psychological, physical, and spiritual pain. I used to run from these, thinking I couldn't cope. My path led me to graduate school and I have been studying toward a doctorate in child psychology for some time now. I want to help those who have been through life's dark side and guide them to where I know there is light."

Michelle is no different from many of us who go blithely along in life without seriously examining who we are or what beliefs we hold. When a tragedy destroys what we believe to be true about life, we are forced to construct anew. This existential loss must also be mourned.

When Marie died, all of Michelle's fears seemed to have come true: fear of loss, fear of the unexpected, fear of the unfamiliar, fear of being unable to cope. Marie's death forced Michelle to confront the unexamined beliefs she had held from childhood and construct her own, based on her own personal reality. Prior to Marie's death, she paid little attention to her internal wisdom, intuition, or natural talents, and placed great value on those of others. Since her vision had been directed toward some nebulous future, she did not often focus on the present.

Paradoxically, once her worst fears materialized, she became less fearful and more willing to take risks. Michelle has developed an appreciation for what is in her life, no longer focusing on what is not. She recognizes that so much of life is out of her control, and yet she trusts in her ability and strength to cope with what life presents. She has the experience to prove it.

Death of an Adult Daughter

Dianna looked forward to having her first grandchild. Her daughter Grace was seven months pregnant. From the obstetrician's office, where she had gone for a routine visit and lab tests, Grace called her mother to say that she was being admitted to the hospital immediately. Leukemia was the diagnosis and the prognosis was bleak. Grace was forced to choose between chemotherapy, with the possible death of the baby, and delaying treatment, which would shorten her own life span.

Even with chemotherapy, the statistics were grim. Grace chose to delay treatment until she was reasonably assured that her baby would be all right. She gave birth to a healthy little girl, Colleen. Three months later Grace died. Dianna's world was no longer the same.

"It's been eighteen years and it's hard to recognize the me that was before her death and the me who is now. Before she died, I was very happy, carefree and secure in the knowledge that I had a comfortable future with my children and grandchild-to-be. My life was orderly and predictable. Whatever I expected usually happened. There were no surprises. Therefore, I was quite secure and complacent. I knew my place in life, I trusted God, and felt secure in the small, safe world of my family. Then Grace died under painfully sad circumstances. Young pregnant women don't get diagnosed with a rapid terminal illness, do they?

"I never knew how destructive grief could be. It took everything I had and what I didn't know I had to make it through. On the other hand, I never knew how constructive it could be.

> "I never knew how destructive grief could be. On the other hand, I never knew how constructive it could be."

"Today, people who don't know me well would say I am the same. Those who know me, and myself most of all, know I am different. I am very aware of how beautiful life is, so I enjoy much more in it. I am appreciative of the smallest things.

"I'm a bit more cautious about those I love. I don't assume they will be there always, so I am grateful for the time I am with them.

"My life's focus has been on my beautiful granddaughter. In this way, I am honoring my daughter's life. Through Colleen I can realize my life's purpose and create meaning from the tragedy of losing my daughter.

"Colleen is truly a magnificent legacy. I have learned that life is about loving and giving from the bounty of that love."

The simplicity and elegance of Dianna's transformation leaves an indelible impression on those who know her. She has distilled the essence of what life is about to three elements: loving, appreciating, and giving. Her self-confidence and self-esteem grew as she worked through the pain and challenges of grief. She learned the pleasure of living in the moment and how to establish and maintain priorities. Her spirituality began to evolve into a real relationship with God rather than knowledge of God as an acquaintance who had been introduced by someone else. Her devotion to her granddaughter has given her a purpose in life and has created a living legacy.

And it came to pass that the group of grievers came upon a site of great devastation where the villagers, their dwelling-huts, and their beasts of burden had all been destroyed by a great flood. And they wondered at the capriciousness of the gods who brought forth gifts of such beauty and wrought calamities of such devastation. And one griever observed: "Such are the ways of this life."

PART TWO: BEREAVEMENT THROUGH CATASTROPHIC CAUSES

Death of a Family

Elizabeth, at the beginning of her retirement years, was just beginning to adapt to life as a widow when, eight days before Christmas, a train–car crash claimed the lives of her daughter, son-in-law, and granddaughter. The sole survivor of that crash was her grandson, Luke, just 14 months old. In a moment, Elizabeth became bereaved mother, bereaved grandmother, and active parent.

"Eight years ago I was free from responsibilities for the first time in my life. My children were independent and I could enjoy a different relationship with them. I was beginning to adapt to widowhood by expanding my interests and network of friends. Others would describe my personality as stubborn, strong-willed, controlling, but also warm and somewhat friendly. I took things as they came. With eight children what else can you do? Life had its ups and downs and losses, but nothing like this tragedy that shattered my life.

"When my daughter, Julia, her husband, and my granddaughter died, my control over everything in life died with them. Never again would I feel the same sense of safety in this world. I'm much more a realist. This doesn't mean that I live in constant fear, but I am more conscious of the hazards of everyday living.

"Even during her life Julia influenced me, though not as profoundly as after she died. She was the essence of goodness in every way. I know . . . most people say that after someone dies, but she really was. Her qualities of compassion, patience, tolerance, and forgiveness are a few of my gifts from her although I haven't perfected tolerance and forgiveness yet.

"I am stronger, wiser, and tougher in all areas from having gone through what no one should experience. Together with Julia's twin, my daughter Ann, I am raising Julia's son. I am devoting my life to fulfilling her role while I am here on earth. My tribute to her is in giving the best possible parenting for this sole survivor of her family. I have gained a bittersweet appreciation for life and all that it holds."

Elizabeth's life was changed in an instant. She was wrenched back into serious responsibilities while grieving incomprehensible losses. Her initial quality of stubbornness grew into the determination that enabled her to tackle overwhelming issues. She incorporated the empathic attributes of her daughter into her own, thus balancing her own strength with Julia's gentleness and compassion.

Elizabeth grew in ways she had never expected. Her determination to co-parent Julia's son gave her a purpose and direction in life. She had to pull back from her retirement dreams and redirect her energy toward another goal. She took on the responsibilities of her deceased daughter with a love and devotion that helped her to create meaning from this senseless loss.

Deaths of a Wife and Child

Gary survived a head-on collision in which his wife Kim and baby daughter Sarah were killed. The driver of the other car, also killed, was drunk and had swerved into Gary's lane.

"In the blink of an eye you find yourself in a twilight zone of hell. From happiness to horror, that's how it was.

"Before Kim and Sarah were killed, I was just a regular kind of guy, concerned with making it big in my engineering firm so I could give my family the best of everything. That is, except for my attention. I worked 12–14 hours a day and had little time left over for them. I thought I was doing the right thing, but I took them for granted. There was always the future, I thought. I'll have time . . . then.

"As head of my firm, I drove others as relentlessly as I did myself. My expectations were outrageous and unrealistic. Tolerance was not my strong suit.

"I went to church on Sunday, as I had been taught, but it was a going-through-the-motions kind of religion. I had no real connection to God.

"Five years later and one hundred years wiser, here I am. Yes, I have grown through this horror and I have softened. Success is not so important anymore; yet, ironically, my business is doing well. I respect those who work for me and that leads to a greater productivity, I guess. I take time for myself now. I have a couple of dogs and they really make me pay attention to physical fitness and nature.

"I want to make a difference in others' lives, not just in my own bank account. I'm active in Big Brothers and I volunteer at the AIDS shelter. I've developed patience and tolerance through the time of grieving. What else could I do but continue to develop, as Kim and Sarah would have wanted me to? I am more than I was in terms of the authentic me and I am less than I was in terms of the artificial me. I will always be thankful for having known and loved Kim and Sarah. I have learned so much about life through their tragic deaths. I wish I could have learned it another way."

> "I have learned so much about life through their tragic deaths. I wish I could have learned it another way."

Gary expresses his growth in a very profound way. Death often takes away the false, pretentious self that we feel is necessary to compete and survive in this world. He describes himself now as a more real human being. His patience with and respect for others is one of the most impressive "gifts" gained from the tragedy. From the bounty of his authentic self, he gives of himself to others. He makes a difference in many lives, including his own.

Death of a Brother

Julian, at 24, was on top of the world with a bright, promising life and career ahead of him. An accident on the ski slopes claimed the life of his younger brother while they were vacationing together.

"My world changed in one split second. Vince's death was the transition point that separated my life into before and after.

"I used to be complacent, reserved, and conventional—some would say passive. My parents and our culture totally defined my self and what I could expect from life. A map of predictable goals stretched out before me. There was not too much in the way of excitement and risk taking, but it was secure and familiar.

"When Vince died, the blueprint for my life was no longer valid. Nothing made sense any more. I became inconsolable and directionless. I returned to work and contained my grief until it could no longer be held in. I was forced to grieve and then began to heal.

"It's ten years later and you asked me to reflect on the changes in me. Well, there are many. I'm my own person now. I make decisions confidently and follow them through. I take risks—oh, nothing life-threatening, just opportunities I would never have thought of taking. I accepted a great job and moved cross-country with my wife one month after our wedding. No one in my family had done such a thing. It wasn't in the blueprint.

"I am committed to lifelong growth. I am very aware of the impermanence of life so I try to live well to honor myself, my family, and the memory of my brother and what he stood for.

"I'm there for those who are most important in my life and I don't take them for granted. I am less concerned with what others think of me because it's what I think of myself and my own integrity that counts.

"I have created meaning from Vince's death by incorporating some of his best qualities into my personality, thereby strengthening and balancing myself. His values and mine combine well as I strive to make a positive difference in others' lives. I matured rapidly albeit painfully after his death and I am forever grateful for his legacy."

His brother's death forced Julian to examine his life, not as others defined it, but as he dreamed of living it. He began to see the possibilities that life offered and no longer took his or anyone else's life for granted. No longer bound by meaningless "rules," he was free to create his own future. His confidence increased in proportion to meeting challenges and making decisions for and by himself. Paradoxically, he was less restricted by fears and felt safer in the world.

Murder of a Son

Ralph was no stranger to grief. He had experienced the deaths of two brothers and two sisters early in his life. He had observed how his mother coped with these tragedies, thereby recording a script for his role in grieving. His firstborn "Tiger," diagnosed with a neuroblastoma at birth, had to have surgery that left him a paraplegic. When Tiger was 23 years old, he was viciously beaten and murdered.

"Before Tiger was murdered, I was more of a loner. A private person by nature, I kept to myself. His death opened up parts of me that are both constructive and destructive. They are powerlessness, frustration, and rage. I've seen and experienced a lot of pain in my life, but nothing like this. The energy of that anger propelled me to seek answers for unanswerable questions and justice. It led me on a mission that has been part of my life for the past eleven years. I sought out others who had been through the same horror. Not finding what I needed, I rounded up others like me and started my own support network.

"The formation of Parents of Murdered Children has opened me up to others. I am less judgmental and take people as I find them. I express my feelings and opinions and that gets me into trouble sometimes. I am a strong advocate for justice in our society. My anger is a tool for change, both for me and for others.

"Our group has funded a memorial garden to be built in a beautiful location in our state capital. It commemorates those children who have been murdered. It speaks volumes against violence and symbolizes peace and beauty.

"Together, we work to bring about a movement toward peace and nonviolence. I can't say it's easy, because redirecting my anger requires great self-discipline and a lot of work. Soon I will say good-bye and goodnight to my beloved son. It is time to put away my commitment to grieving him. It is time for me to live without him."

A self-proclaimed loner, Ralph became more open to people and empathic with their pain. He became more tolerant and compassionate. He allowed himself to receive as well as give comfort and support. Meeting the challenges of grieving the death of his son increased his self-confidence and self-esteem.

His love and appreciation for the loved ones in his life became more of a conscious awareness and prioritizing them in his life became a living commitment. The violence of his son's death propelled him toward a movement toward peace and nonviolence. His rage fueled the changes in his relationships with others, his beliefs and spirituality, and his ultimate personal growth. In this way he was able to create meaning from the tragedy.

Suicide of a Son

Hope felt that she had everything she expected to have in life: three children in their teens, a comfortable job, a stable marriage, and a nice home. This was the way it was supposed to be and it was, at least until New Year's Eve, when her youngest son, Eric, age 16, killed himself with a shotgun.

"Before Eric died, I was satisfied with what life had presented. I was basically a positive person with an upbeat attitude. I thought I was grown up, mature and living out the 'happily ever after' part of my life. I went along with others' plans and decisions, not really considering my own. I didn't realize I had any goals other than those of my family. My family was everything to me; all else was window trimming.

"When this tragedy fractured my little porcelain model of the world, it wouldn't fit. I was disoriented. I no longer knew who I was, what my roles were, or what to do next.

"The years afterward brought pain, suffering, and nothing *but* change and growth. My life surged forward but my marriage didn't. It was another casualty in the aftermath of my son's death.

"During my grief I realized I could withstand this pain and that I would create a meaning from his death so that it would not have occurred in vain. I was committed to living the best possible life that was within my control.

"As I struggled onward, my self-confidence increased as I tried out new choices and new behaviors. I returned to school to try to understand the psychology of what Eric had done. I found so much more.

"I began a new career which has led me to satisfaction, success, and fulfillment. I am helping others in a way I never imagined was possible. I'm making a difference in people's lives and helping them through their pain.

"My self-esteem increased as I began to take better care of myself. I really hadn't done that before, so concerned was I with the health and welfare of everyone else.

"With the changes in me came a new dimension in my ability to be compassionate, tolerant, and thoughtful. My capacity for being in a mature relationship led to the fulfilling one I have now. My relationships with my children and grandchildren are rich with love and laughter.

"I am my own independent yet interdependent woman. The fullness of my life is a testimony to my son's brief life and tragic death. He would be proud of me."

Before her son's death, Hope had encountered few decisions or challenges, so she had little occasion to take risks and thereby develop her self-confidence and self-esteem. She drifted along without direction until catastrophe struck. Her nature was optimistic and that gave her the strength she needed to get started in transforming her life. From the depths of her pain and at her lowest moment, she chose to better her life by helping others, thus creating meaning from the life and tragic death of her youngest son.

Murder of a Daughter

David was a successful government executive. He, his wife, and daughter were accustomed to living in a predictable, sheltered environment. He had a blueprint for the future which did not include a tragedy: the murder of his 19-year-old daughter Ruth.

"I reflect on what I was like before that devastating event and I see a man in control, driven to compete and succeed in life, which was not terribly unusual for most men of my generation. My focal point in life was my career and I paid little attention to the emotional needs of my family; providing for them financially was my perceived role.

"My concern was not in helping others in an altruistic way. I interacted with people in a respectful manner but without true empathy. I was rather intolerant and impatient, mostly because I felt a sense of urgency to get things accomplished. I did not reveal my true inner feelings to anyone, especially at work. That would have exposed my vulnerability and would not have helped me in my competitive arena.

"When my daughter, Ruth, was murdered, I could not mentally or emotionally accept it. It just could not be made real. For a long while I locked it up inside me and buried myself in activities, hoping the pain and grief would go away. They did not. Instead, the pressure built up and finally erupted. I was diagnosed as being clinically depressed and sought help for dealing with my denial. It took many years, eight or more, to be able to integrate the experience of losing Ruth and in so violent a manner.

"Today, I try to be open and honest in my feelings, both to myself and to others. I am retired now and have balanced my life with some quiet, introspective pursuits and some that are quite the opposite.

"A few years after Ruth's death, circumstances (fate?) led me to become a volunteer in a prison where I began to heal and grow through participating with the prisoners on religious fellowship. How ironic! Also, I began holding workshops of the Alternatives to Violence (AVP) program to help society through helping the inmates learn other methods of discharging aggression. Then I led support groups and assisted in some of the inmates' transitions from prison to home. I found more than I expected to find and certainly have received so much.

"Through working with these groups, I have come to forgive the man who killed my daughter, not condoning his crime, mind you, but letting it go and moving on. I am no longer imprisoned by feelings of anger, grief, or guilt. I have received the most valuable 'gifts' from this tragedy and often, as I enter the locked steel gates of the prison, I look up at the sky and say a silent prayer to my daughter, 'This is for you, Ruth.' "

David is a strong, serene man who radiates warmth and acceptance. He speaks honestly and courageously of his imperfections: the rigidity and compulsive drive to succeed that constituted his personality before the death of his daughter. His self-image was modeled after society's description of the successful man. Introspection was an unavailable luxury. Empathy and compassion did not form part of his job description and hence he was unable to truly understand his daughter during her brief life. It is one of his deepest regrets.

David has grown in many ways and considers these new aspects of his personality to be gifts. His compassion and unconditional acceptance of his fellow human beings are self-generated through the pain of his grief and externally reciprocated from his work with the prisoners. He is also active in community, political, and self-help groups. David lives his spirituality through his altruistic works. He is an active participant in his church. He extends the love in his heart to those in need at all levels, not judging, not asking for anything in return. He reveres the memory of his daughter and creates meaning from her tragic death by bringing comfort, forgiveness and hope to those in despair.

Suicide of a Daughter; Death of a Husband

Eleven years ago, Joyce was the proud mother of a son and daughter and the devoted wife of a loving, gentle man. A domino effect began when her daughter Mary, age 20, committed suicide. Then Joyce lost her job. Her grief-stricken husband Maurice, 44 years old, suffered a stroke shortly afterward and died of a heart attack two years later.

"Before my daughter Mary died, I was very controlling. I worked as a research scientist and believed that it was possible to mold people and events. I was unaccustomed to feelings of powerlessness and helplessness since I assumed control over most situations. My family of origin was not a demonstrative or communicative one. This was my role model for dealing with adversity. I isolated myself and did not reach out to others to share or receive. It was the only way I knew.

"The deaths of Mary and Maurice were huge lessons in powerlessness. It was proof that I was not in control and had never been in control. I simply did not have the power to have intervened or prevented their deaths.

"Now, several years later, I am a much more sensitive person as a result of Mary and Maurice's deaths. I have learned to accept myself as less than flawless. I do the best that I can but don't expect to do everything perfectly.

"I am very active in the Compassionate Friends Society and have been a chapter leader for many years, now on a national level. I feel less helpless if I can help others deal with their losses.

It is when we have nothing to contribute that we feel the most helpless. I am content with my new place in the world as I continue to reach out to help others.

"I am a different person and strongly committed to creating a meaningful life for myself. I look for ways to serve others that nourish me at the same time. I can see more clearly now what is important in life."

Joyce let go of her beliefs about controlling events and people. She redefined what she actually had power over and began to direct her efforts there. She became more sensitive and open to others, giving as well as receiving. She found her role models in the men and women who exemplified the philosophy of the Compassionate Friends.

Through her unselfish giving of time, Joyce became more than she was before. She strengthened aspects of her self as well as her interactions with others. She learned to be more fully human while creating meaning from the premature deaths of her daughter and husband. She became the role model she had been looking for in others.

Sequential Deaths

Megan, 35 years old, a happily married businesswoman, felt in charge of her life, blissfully unaware of the deaths to come. The first was her husband's to cancer, the next, her beloved father's, and then, a few years later her fiancé's, also to cancer.

"I never realized how innocent I was to life's tragedies. I was always planning the future according to my view of it. There was evidently another version. I went through all the terror of grief with each death. It was not easy or comfortable. I knew it had to be done. Each death prepared me to handle the next. For this, I am grateful.

"I am a stronger person for having loved and lost those wonderful men. I am more aware of my capacity to love and understand others. I can honestly face my fears and limitations. I no longer overreact to problems. To some degree I plan only for the present, not the future, that is, over the things I can control.

> "I am a stronger person for having loved and lost those wonderful men."

"You might say I have learned what is important and what isn't, and this truly guides my path in life. I appreciate what life has to offer. Sure, I'm wary of loving again, but it will not stop me from continuing to love and love deeply."

This remarkable young woman is well past the disruptive phases of grief. She is aware of her feelings and expresses them well. Megan has a very strong sense of self, coupled with the confidence in her own ability to handle what comes her way. She is more focused on the present moment and appreciates what she has in life. She knows that she will allow herself the gift of love in the future. Megan is a stronger woman with more maturity and wisdom than many who are much older. She is admired and respected by those who know her.

SUMMARY

- Grief can accelerate advancement through developmental levels through revolution rather than evolution.
- How we use the opportunities and challenges of bereavement is crucial to healing and growth.
- The Phoenix Grievers are role models for transformation through grief.
- Phoenix Grievers' transformations took place in four areas of change: the self, relationships with others, the physical world, and the spiritual world.

The little band of grievers finally found those who would guide them on their pilgrimage toward healing and hope. They prepared for the journey....

4

Into the Fire:
Phase One—Impact

And as they traveled, they felt dazed. They shuffled ahead as if they were in a trance....

Of all the incomprehensible concepts of life, the death of a loved one is the most alien. When people are confronted with the news of a beloved's death, they must wrestle with the foreign concept for a time in order to familiarize themselves with its parameters. This is akin to the disorientation of the little band of grievers about to set forth on their odyssey through the unfamiliar terrain of grief.

Several protective mechanisms are released to defend the griever from the invasion of familiar territory. They are shock, denial, and disbelief. Initially the defenses are helpful. Later, they function as barriers to the continuation of the journey. They must eventually be dissolved in order for the griever to move onward. This is the mission of the first phase of grief, *Impact*.

A STRANGE NEW WORLD

The griever has just learned that a loved one has died. The stunned individual recoils from the force of the news.

| Impact | Chaos | Adaptation | Equilibrium | Transformation |

A sensation of unreality ensues and some feel as if they were in a "foreign space." This space is the habitat where grief begins, where people and events are perceived differently. Reality is shattered and time is forever divided into before and after.

Phase One
Impact
A Strange New World
Shock
Denial
Holding On
Creating Meaning

Even the perception of the self is strange. The griever feels functionally robotic, unable to cope. Unfortunately, at this time, there are many responsibilities confronting the griever that demand concentration and decision making. So it is that the self splits: the robotic part attempts to stabilize and do what needs to be done; the other part continues to feel dazed and numb. The disoriented griever, fearful of the future, tightens her grip on the past and tries to cope in the present.

Michelle had responsibilities to her son, the surviving twin, and to her husband. She relates: "There is a part of me just going through the motions of everyday life. The other part of me is stuck in the past."

The mourner feels confused as she tries to retrieve the comforting feeling of life as it was before the loss. Bewilderment complicates the desperate struggle to regain self-control. All that was familiar is now alien and the once-known world no longer exists.

Joyce, whose daughter committed suicide and whose husband died soon afterward, recalls: "Nothing in my life had any stability; nothing was the same as before their deaths. I could not believe the same philosophies. I could not trust life in the same way. I was permanently altered in a profound and disconcerting way. I no longer fit into the world as I had known it."

Impact	Chaos	Adaptation	Equilibrium	Transformation

Joyce expresses what so many bereaved individuals feel: that the world is radically changed. As we go through life, we assume certain things to be consistent about our world. Parkes (1971) refers to this collection of beliefs as "the assumptive world." This describes a concept we hold in our minds about ourselves, our place in the world, and the "rules" that allow us to navigate through this life with a sense of security and continuity.

These assumptions allow us to incorporate information from life, interpret what it means to us, and place it within the congruent framework of our handbook for living. This viewpoint arises from several factors: family, society, religion, peers, and our basic personality structure. Our assumptive world contributes to what we expect to experience in life as a consequence of certain behaviors; the quid pro quo of life.

Gary, bereaved husband and father, describes his assumptive world. He felt that "If I did all the right things, and was good to my fellow man, nothing bad was going to happen to me or my family. It was a kind of insurance policy that I felt guaranteed us protection from catastrophe." Death forced him to confront his assumptions as he asked himself, "How could I have been so naive?"

The death of a loved one is not part of the bargain that one has made with God or any other perceived higher authority. A feeling of betrayal surfaces when the "contract" is broken, and the loss plays havoc with the griever's trust and belief system. Death is a betrayal of our covenant with life. When the mourner's long-held beliefs are fractured, confusion, anxiety, and fear begin to develop. Most often, the griever is initially protected from these emotions, through the mechanism of shock.

| Impact | Chaos | Adaptation | Equilibrium | Transformation |

SHOCK

The psychological blow of learning of a loved one's death can be so overwhelming that the mind rushes to shield the griever. One protective mechanism is shock. Shock incorporates several phenomena, such as numbness, disbelief, and disorientation. Grievers experience a kind of emotional novocaine, which numbs the mind and psyche from unbearable pain. The impact of grief can be powerful enough to render both psychological and physical shock to an individual. A griever may collapse completely.

> Grievers experience a kind of emotional novocaine, which numbs the mind and psyche from unbearable pain.

Rachel, a young woman whose husband suffered a sudden and fatal stroke at work, said, "Sam's boss came to the backyard where I was gardening and told me that he had bad news, that Sam had died. I heard the words but they didn't connect and I tried to go to him. The next thing I knew I woke up in my bed. I guess I fainted. I cried, but only a little. I felt frozen and numb. This helped because there were arrangements that needed to be made and it allowed me to make them."

Stronger elements of shock, disbelief, and denial are more probable in cases of sudden bereavement. The "two U's" apply to these situations, *unexpected* and *unprepared*. When the death of a loved one is unexpected, the griever is unprepared. The reaction is immediate. There is no choice: a crisis state ensues, and the griever must react or respond. Even shock or denial is a response. Often there is no time for gradually assimilating the news.

Many grievers report feeling as if a transparent wall had been placed between them and the rest of the world. They

| Impact | Chaos | Adaptation | Equilibrium | Transformation |

could hear and see others but felt dissociated from them. Many experience a feeling of alienation from the "normal" world. Grievers may feel isolated from the familiar patterns of daily life as they existed before the impact.

It is not unusual for a mourner to feel different from their peers after the death of a loved one. This difference may lead to negative definitions about the self. One young widow described her experience as a feeling of shame. "I know it was irrational but I felt that I had done something wrong and somehow others looked at me with censure. I only know that I felt very different, like a pariah." Feelings of shame are intensified in situations involving deaths by suicide or murder.

David, whose daughter was murdered, felt severe pangs of shame. He remarks, "In the State Department, conformity was the norm. Anything outside of that made one feel different. This act of violence against my daughter was not something I could share freely and openly with my colleagues. I didn't know how to respond and ask for help. It was as if I had done something wrong."

In attempting to understand the baffling circumstances surrounding a death others may rationalize the trauma. By defining their own version of cause and effect, they can control the danger. This pseudo-control mechanism offers little protection against harm.

For instance, if someone were killed in a motorcycle accident, others might identify the motorcycle as the cause of the death and thus avoid motorcycle riding. Others might conclude that the deceased or the family was to blame somehow for the tragedy. "If they hadn't done such and such or if she had done something differently, this wouldn't have happened." These things are not meant maliciously. Rather they are our

| Impact | Chaos | Adaptation | Equilibrium | Transformation |

psyche's way of trying to distance and insulate us from a similar happening through the illusion that we can control our fate by conscious deliberation and action.

Grievers who are experiencing shock and dissociation may appear to function well. They often conduct themselves with dignity, composure, and strength. Yet after the rituals are over, these grievers may have little or no recollection of what they or anyone else did or said. Their protective numbness insulated them from reality.

Barbara, a widow, remembers having to take care of her mother and Mike's parents during and after the funeral. She focused on their needs. "I was the perfect caregiver. It gave me a purpose for a time, to make sure everyone else was okay. The downside of this was that they stabilized and I crashed into a wall of grief by myself."

Many individuals hold these strong, responsible roles in their families and not only do others expect their stability, they also demand it of themselves. These grievers need to be aware of the need to grieve following a postponement. If they realize that they are making a tradeoff by delaying their acute grief for a short period of time, then they may effectively tend to their own grief very soon afterward.

Shock is usually most intense in the time span immediately following the news of the death. However, elements of shock, disbelief, and disorientation may present intermittently for several weeks afterward. And there are those who suffer multiple losses and remain in a state of shock for a longer period of time.

Joyce, who lost her daughter, her job, and then her husband, all within a two-year time frame says, "For a while I imagined there was a curse on me that so many bad things were hap-

| Impact | Chaos | Adaptation | Equilibrium | Transformation |

pening: Mary's suicide, losing my job, Maurice's stroke, followed by his heart attack and then his death. It was impossible to recover from one blow before the next hit. I stayed in shock for a long time."

Additional crisis situations may contribute to a more intense and prolonged grieving process. These circumstances contain a "crisis within a crisis." They are overwhelming for even the strongest and most emotionally healthy of us. In such instances the individual is encouraged to seek treatment from someone skilled in grief counseling and therapy.

DENIAL

The protective mechanism of denial occurs most often during the initial phase of grief. It is the mind's attempt to stabilize the griever's shattered world by rejecting the actuality of the death. Protest reactions ("It can't be true," and "I can't believe this") are attempts to hold back the reality of the death to allow the mind time to absorb the facts.

Grievers often maintain the hope that someone will come and tell them that it was all a mistake, a dream, a nightmare. Worden (1991) states, "After a death, it is very normal to hope for a reunion or to assume that the deceased is not gone" (p. 12). Mourners often express the feeling that they were having a nightmare from which they would soon wake up.

Denial can be a valiant attempt to restore balance. It allows grievers to acclimate to the altered circumstances of their lives and carry on their routines. Denial may operate subconsciously or it may actually be chosen as a way to cope with the phase of Impact. Regardless, it should be used judiciously, as in this griever's attempt to postpone the emotional components of her loss.

| Impact | Chaos | Adaptation | Equilibrium | Transformation |

Noella, the young widow whose husband Bob had died five years after suffering a stroke, was one of the strong ones. She was left with two small children. "I had to keep going. There was no time to grieve. I felt that my total energy must be directed toward providing a home and earning a living for my boys. Anything else was out of the question."

Many grievers can relate to Noella's choice to consciously compartmentalize grief in order to stabilize a crisis situation. This is not a denial that a death has occurred but rather a postponement of the imperative to express the emotional consequences of the loss.

A hazard exists in delaying grief. Grievers may find themselves alone with unleashed suffering long after others have moved on. Refusing to feel the natural reactions to the death of someone beloved puts off healing and may precipitate a range of emotional and/or physical illnesses. Grief's energy is powerful and needs to be expressed.

Minimizing the loss in order to feel less pain is another form of denial. The premise is that if the deceased is remembered in a negative way, or if the relationship is devalued, then grief can be lessened or extinguished. Grievers trick themselves in this way to avoid the pain of the full implications of someone's death.

Carole, 20 years old, was the youngest of five children. After the death of her father, who indulged and spoiled her, she said, "I told myself and others that it was time for me to grow up and this [his death] was a good thing that happened. My father was too controlling, too protective for me to try anything on my own that wasn't approved by him.

"It was a long time before I could feel the pain of losing everything that was good about him and his love for me. I realized that I needed to grieve all of it and I made myself do it.

| Impact | Chaos | Adaptation | Equilibrium | Transformation |

It took some work and some therapy, but I did it and it helped me through the denial and what his death meant to my life."

Carole's insight into her relationship with her father altered. Her need to grieve "all of it" propelled her into therapy. She made a deliberate choice to begin the process of grieving, and, as a result, she was able to integrate the whole relationship into her psyche.

Physical evidence of the death helps grievers to get past denial. The mind needs to be nudged over and over to absorb the devastating fact. Viewing the body of the loved one, touching the face or hands, smoothing the hair, serve as sensory stimuli to help acknowledge that the death has occurred, thus toppling the barriers of shock, denial, and disbelief.

Amy's twin brother Jeffrey, age 19, was killed in an automobile accident while she was vacationing in Europe. "I could not and would not believe that it was my brother who died. It was impossible. When I got home from my vacation, I would find out they had made a mistake.

"It took me a long time to absorb his death. I needed to see him, and I did—in the funeral home. I saw his face, so much like mine, I held his hand and smoothed his hair. I looked and touched and talked, until my mind, not my heart, believed it was Jeff lying there, dead. My heart caught up much later."

We may be doubting Thomases when it comes to accepting something without any proof. Funerals and other rituals help grievers overcome the aspects of unreality that accompany the death of a loved one. It is difficult to deny that a death has occurred when a ritual is commemorating that very fact. A death not validated is a postponement of the natural sequence of grief.

Impact	Chaos	Adaptation	Equilibrium	Transformation

HOLDING ON

Individuals feel a desperate need to re-experience the sensation of being with the loved one. They seek temporary comfort in something that affirms the felt presence of the loved one. Revisiting a favorite place, listening to favorite music, sniffing the beloved's clothing, looking at photographs or other objects all make grievers feel connected to their beloved once again.

Sarah was 12 when her mother died. For years she fell asleep holding her mother's bathrobe. "I knew it was silly but it comforted me and made me feel close to her. My therapist explained that this was natural and I began to feel better about it. It took years for me to let go of that robe and now it's hanging in my closet for when I need it."

Other grievers may visit the grave and talk to their loved one for comfort and relief. Many feel able to verbalize their feelings to a nonjudgmental presence. The ritual may continue for a long while and may even become incorporated into the griever's life. This form of connection may serve a positive psychological purpose. It becomes a link to the deceased while the griever is acknowledging the death.

Scott, whose father committed suicide, would frequently stop by the cemetery to "let go of what was on my mind that day. I could let out my anger, frustration, whatever I wanted. It was such a release, especially in the beginning when I could not believe he was really dead."

There are others who prefer not go to the cemetery or gravesite. They find no peace or comfort. They feel no link with their loved one there. This choice is highly personal and should be respected.

| Impact | Chaos | Adaptation | Equilibrium | Transformation |

Many grievers report dreams or visions in which they see or hear their loved ones or feel their presence. This does not mean the griever is going crazy, although many may feel that way. These sensory impressions can be frightening, and individuals need to be reassured that they are not uncommon when and if they occur.

CREATING MEANING

Creating meaning from a tragedy means activating a process I call *spiritual alchemy*. This term describes the process of transforming something hurtful into something beneficial. Spiritual alchemy is a way of creating meaning from a loved one's death. This choice provides grievers an opportunity to create meaning from the death of their loved ones and at the same time honor their lives.

> Spiritual alchemy is a way of creating meaning from a loved one's death.

It is important to realize that the phase of Impact offers the vulnerable griever limited options for creating meaning. The work of grief demands the full capacity of the mourner's time, energy, and focus. The needs of the individual take precedence over everything else. If doing something meaningful enhances the person's resources, fine. If not, alchemy may be postponed until the grief process has advanced further. The fourth and fifth phases of grief, Equilibrium and Transformation, will offer plenty of opportunities for creating meaning.

Seeing the opportunities arising from the death of a loved one distinguishes a Phoenix Griever from others. They may

- create something *tangibly* beneficial for others from the loved one's death

| Impact | Chaos | Adaptation | Equilibrium | Transformation |

- create something *symbolically* beneficial for the intrapersonal self
- create something *altruistically* beneficial from the transformed self to help others.

Thus, the benefits increase exponentially as they pass from the deceased through the griever to many others, directly or indirectly. Creating meaning from a loved one's death is one of the most elegant expressions of our ability to transcend adversity.

> Creating meaning from a loved one's death is one of the most elegant expressions of our ability to transcend adversity.

Tangible benefits

One example of tangible benefits is the donation of organs. The sharing of body parts is one of the most life enhancing of all gifts. The mourner decides, as agent for the deceased, to do something to create meaning from a tragedy otherwise devoid of benefit.

Patty, whose husband was killed when she was pregnant, donated her husband's kidneys and liver to the transplant program. "Although I was in shock and couldn't truly realize what a gift this was, I knew it would be the only immediate unselfish gesture he could make, through me. I knew this was something that truly reflected the humanistic qualities of my husband."

Phoenix Grievers are often operating on a subconscious level when they create something meaningful while they are still experiencing shock and disbelief. Yet, they are instinctively drawn to the life-affirming decisions in which they will

| Impact | Chaos | Adaptation | Equilibrium | Transformation |

later derive comfort. It is important to understand that not all Phoenix Grievers have the opportunity or inclination to create meaning in this way, at this time. Religious, ethical, or personal thinking may govern their choices and should be respected.

Rae Ann's daughter, 16-year-old Kayla, was killed in a motor vehicle accident. Rae Ann has since given of her time and energy to the organ donor program. She says, "I have always believed in the organ donor program and I find that I have received a blessing in the midst of this tragedy. Kayla's organs gave eight others a second chance for life, a new beginning for them and their families. . . . organ donation gave us the strength to find some peace when our whole world crashed."

Establishing a conduit for financial contributions can be another tangible way to create meaning. It may take the form of a scholarship, a donation to a philanthropic or religious organization, or a fund designated for a particular helpful purpose like endowing a chair at a university in the loved one's memory. Other examples are statues, memorials, gardens, or other visual creations. Most mourners derive comfort from honoring their loved ones' memories. The griever becomes the facilitator in a tangible manifestation of spiritual alchemy.

Symbolic benefits

Rituals create meaning during the transition from before to after. They help isolate and accentuate a notable event. Rando (personal interview 1998) says, "Rituals serve two purposes, the need for expression of feelings about the de-

| Impact | Chaos | Adaptation | Equilibrium | Transformation |

ceased and the need to distinguish the transition of death."
She offers the example of roadside crosses placed at the sites
of fatalities. The markers announce that a tragic event took
place there.

Rituals allow grievers to take some form of action, thus
alleviating some of the powerlessness they feel about a loved
one's death. Mourners feel the need to do something with their
frustration and pain. Rando (1993) explains, "Rituals also
promote physical release, which decreases intensity of emotion, promotes clearer thinking, and discharges pent-up tension" (p. 315).

Rituals may take the form of communications to the deceased. One young woman wrote letters to her mother and
put them in the mailbox with no address. Another tucked
messages into the earth by the beloved's grave. At the
graveside of my beloved godson, Kevin, who died when I was
completing this book, the children released white balloons to
the sky to say good-bye and send their love.

The parents of a 12-year-old boy who died offered a unique
and compassionate ritual for grief expression. They created
a web page on the Internet so that his friends could share
their feelings about his death and their grief. Their notes
animated him anew for his family and comforted other class-
mates who logged on, while providing a sensitive forum for
them to express their emotions to and about him.

Altruistic benefits

These sophisticated and benevolent gestures are most frequently evidenced in the latter phases of grief, Adaptation,
Equilibrium and Transformation. They will be further eluci-
dated in later chapters.

| Impact | Chaos | Adaptation | Equilibrium | Transformation |

GRIEF WORK

During this phase the mourner needs to acknowledge that the loved one is dead. One cannot fully grieve and move forward without acknowledging the death. Believing does not mean accepting. Acceptance takes a longer period of time.

Impact allows the griever to gradually assimilate the reality of the death while numbed by the emotional novocaine of shock. The mechanisms of denial and disbelief push away the truth and hold it at an objective distance while the mind struggles to allow the unthinkable to be thought. The elements of the Impact phase combine to enable the mind to protest and then absorb the formidable reality of a loved one's death. After mourners affirm the reality of death, they are challenged to collapse the barriers of shock, denial, and disbelief.

As the death is becoming more and more real, the emotions that follow are intense. They herald the beginning of the second phase of grief, Chaos. Before we explore that, we will consider the Phoenix Grievers' recommendations based on their experiences of what was helpful during Impact.

FOR THE GRIEVER

Phoenix Grievers recommend:

- Establish an eating, sleeping, and resting routine as soon as possible.
- Do only what you have to do during the immediate days after the death. Focus on one thing at a time.
- Reach out for support from family, friends, neighbors, co-workers.

| Impact | Chaos | Adaptation | Equilibrium | Transformation |

- Get help with decisions such as funeral arrangements, legal and other matters.
- Call your physician to schedule a touch-base appointment.
- Take time off to grieve and to rest and replenish yourself.
- Expect to feel stunned. Be easy on yourself.
- Express your feelings to trusted others. Tell your story over and over. Do not feel guilty for taking up their time and attention.
- Help dependent others with their grief (children, the elderly). Get help with this if necessary.
- Use self-talk to encourage yourself and lessen your fears.
- Consider seeing a grief counselor/therapist for information and guidance.
- Know that you will make it through. Never let go of hope!

FOR THE THERAPIST

The initial Impact phase breaks down the griever's perceptual world, sending the person sliding down the pyramid of functionality into a state of crisis and regressing to the base of Maslow's (1970) hierarchy of needs. "Even the healthy and strong will plummet to a realistic level of defense against the threat to one's safety and security (p. 43)." Using a developmental framework, the therapist assesses the griever's degree of functioning and quickly strategizes a plan to restore the individual to a stable level. This in no way implies that the griever's world is as it previously was.

Therapists should utilize a variation of the crisis model of intervention. (See Table 4–1.) The griever's physiological and safety needs are priorities. Very little will be accomplished if

| Impact | Chaos | Adaptation | Equilibrium | Transformation |

the griever has not been eating, sleeping, or establishing a modicum of structure in a chaotic environment. The griever's physical needs must be stabilized as quickly as possible. A plan to restore homeostasis should be delineated during the first session. The therapist's role is more active during the first three phases of grief than in later stages.

Table 4–1. The Phoenix Model of Grief: Impact

Needs	Tasks	Intervention
For:	*To:*	*Use:*
Food, shelter, rest, sleep	Maintain physiological stability	Crisis intervention in a humanistic manner
Safety and security	Establish security and safety measures	Directive approach (griever is stunned and decision making may be difficult)
Preliminary belonging	Assimilate the reality of the death; reach out to supportive others	Creativity in designing a support team; guidance toward community resources

Therapists should have a written information sheet describing the model of grief, its signs and symptoms, and signs of distress. The support team should include the therapist as well as others such as family, friends, co-workers, physician, support group persons, clergy, and any other relevant helpers.

Grievers need to recover structure and security as quickly as possible. Therefore, a realistic plan with realistic alternatives should be co-created during the first session. Based on an accurate evaluation, it will include what to expect during this phase of grief and how to handle it, whom to contact and

| Impact | Chaos | Adaptation | Equilibrium | Transformation |

how, and when to notify the therapist or physician, These proactive measures will ensure that signs of trouble are quickly identified and treated.

Psychologist Dr. Catherine Sanders (1989) states: "If the bereaved individual is nurtured and tended to as one would tend any shock victim, chances for a less abrasive bereavement are strengthened" (p. 51). This statement certainly applies to the Impact phase of grief and is a very important theme to keep in mind. The griever needs to be nurtured. The baseline needs must be filled. The Phoenix Model is designed to move the griever forward in the process of grief.

It is essential that the griever talk about the death over and over in order to make it real. Saying the words and hearing them appear to have beneficial capabilities. Pennebacker (1990) believes that expressing inhibited emotions through language (putting them into words) helps individuals to understand and absorb the event. Articulation of the facts is crucial to the breakdown of denial. The mourner has to hear, interpret, and comprehend the unthinkable news. Information about the meaning of the loss will begin to be revealed as the therapist hears the griever's story of the death.

Grief confronts the mourner's senses when the loved one is no longer seen, heard, smelled, or touched. Coping with these physical deprivations may be eased by the presence of supportive others who respond to the individual's need to express denial and disbelief.

The therapist should be skilled in grief counseling and therapy. In addition, a warm, humanistic and nonjudgmental manner will help the griever feel safe and understood. Attending to the safety needs also means addressing the anxiety and fear that emerge during the latter part of this phase. Providing information about grief, establishing a support network, and structuring a realistic plan will advance the process.

| Impact | Chaos | Adaptation | Equilibrium | Transformation |

Death creates its own unique set of consequences for each individual. For example, the death of a child in the family will have different repercussions than the death of the "breadwinner." The therapist is advised to begin to understand what the death means to the griever even though the existential meaning may not surface until later. Chapters 7 and 8 will address grievers' perceptions of the death of a loved one and how their beliefs influence their grief process.

Some suggestions for therapists during this phase are:

- **Listen:** Hear the griever's story with your ears, eyes, and heart, with compassion, empathy, and patience. Let your therapeutic self be the observer while you are "in the experience" with the griever.
- **Assess:** Use the Phoenix Model as a guide to assess the griever's psychological, physical, and behavioral needs. Always ask about suicidality if you suspect that it might be a factor.
- **Normalize:** Give the griever a handout of the grief model and, very briefly, describe where he or she is in the process. Use the griever's own words in describing his or her feelings.
- **Reassure:** Let the griever know that he/she will be able to go through the process and that guidance and support are available.
- **Support:** Connect the griever to support networks in the family, among friends, neighbors, co-workers, clergy, and groups (self-help and professional). Beware of isolation.
- **Plan:** Formulate realistic goals. Do not overwhelm the griever. Prioritize physiological and safety needs during this phase. Partner with the griever to design a short-term plan.

| Impact | Chaos | Adaptation | Equilibrium | Transformation |

- **Clarify:** Elucidate each party's expectations and agree on short-term goals and frequency of visits. Suggest that the individual make an appointment with his/her physician to monitor health status.

SUMMARY

- The initial phase of grief is called Impact.
- Impact is composed of shock, denial, and disbelief, which act as emotional novocaine to a griever.
- The "grief work" of this phase is to acknowledge that the death of a loved one has occurred.
- "Grief work" liberates a griever to move forward in the grief process, thus facilitating healing and growth.

And the trance began to lift and feelings were gradually restored to the grievers and the feelings were not what they had hoped for. . . .

| Impact | Chaos | Adaptation | Equilibrium | Transformation |

5

The Challenge:
Phase Two—Chaos

And many were overcome with emotion, yet others struggled to contain their grief. The grievers continued on and came to a village where a large fenced-in area contained several horses. And all were prancing about, save one, who lay in a corner. . . .

The emotional novocaine is wearing off, leaving the griever vulnerable to the emotional and physical repercussions of grief. This phase challenges grievers to be aware that their symptoms are characteristic of the aftermath of losing a loved one. Once such awareness is established, grievers feel less anxious about their own stability. Awareness opens the door to acknowledgment, which leads to acceptance of what follows. The ideal outcome of this continuum and an important objective of this phase is the expression of the painful thoughts and emotions of grief. This is often blocked by grievers' defense mechanisms.

CRAZY TIMES

As the emotional numbing of shock is wearing off, the griever begins to confront the painful emotions of loss. Many find this

| Impact | Chaos | Adaptation | Equilibrium | Transformation |

phase to be the most intense, even though it is one of the briefest passages in the continuum of grief. Grievers frequently say they feel like they are going crazy.

Phase Two
Chaos
Crazy Times
Anxiety and Fear
Powerlessness
Guilt
Anger
Depression
Alienation

Joyce, bereaved mother and widow recalls: "I wish I had known some of the symptoms of grief, the ups and downs, the sleepless nights, the hallucinations, the obsessions. I believed I was losing my mind and was afraid to talk about it to others for fear of being labeled crazy. Perhaps if I had known more about normal grief. . . ."

This crazy time will often elicit the question "How long am I going to feel like this?" This query reveals the griever's fear of not being able to handle the suffering, which seems interminable.

Grief has a time line of its own and each person's behavior along the span is different. To ease anxiety the griever should be reminded that the intense pain is part of the briefest of the phases of grief. Even though emotional distress periodically and episodically surfaces throughout the course of grieving, the acute phase can be managed with guidance, support, and understanding. The experiences of the Phoenix Grievers contribute to that understanding.

Maggie, whose husband Ted died after a protracted death trajectory, says of time: "I believe how long it takes is different for everyone. Grieving is a process and continues probably for as long as there is life and memory. You will always miss the one you love. However, after a couple of years you begin embracing the joys of life again. Even in the darkest days, the small joys are always there because they are what get you through."

Impact	Chaos	Adaptation	Equilibrium	Transformation

The Phoenix Grievers appreciate that grief and joy are ongoing, integral, intertwined parts of life. Although they may have originally assumed that grief has a beginning, middle, and end, they have come to learn that the aftermath of losing a loved one is woven into the fabric of their lives. Mourning a loved one becomes part of who we are. Life itself is a continuing series of experiences of joy and sorrow.

> Mourning a loved one becomes part of who we are.

Ann, whose mother died six years earlier, describes the ongoing process of missing her mother: "I am done grieving. Yes, I miss my mother and get sad sometimes because she's not around, but I don't want that to stop. I feel like that keeps her near to me. So you need the bad along with the good."

Ann defines her grief as over, yet goes on to redefine grieving as a process of integrating the memory of her mother into her life. She has established a new and positive relationship with her mother.

The consequences of grief during Chaos lead mourners to ask, "What's wrong with me?" Thoughts cannot be followed through. Concentration is muddled. Memory deficits occur.

Michelle remembers: "My thoughts were out of control. I obsessed over everything: my health, my family's heath, fears about losing another person I love, and fears about nameless, impending doom.

"I had difficulty focusing on any one thing. It felt like my brain was short-circuiting. Finally, with some medication, therapy, and using the thought techniques I had learned, I was able to manage some of the runaway thoughts and fears. It took a lot of self-discipline and work, but it was effective. When I had trouble concentrating or couldn't remember simple things, I didn't push

| Impact | Chaos | Adaptation | Equilibrium | Transformation |

myself. I kept saying to myself that this would pass and that I could do it."

Phoenix Grievers found that self-talk helped them manage the fearful obsessing. Those who were fortunate enough to be acquainted with normal grief were able to understand the memory and concentration deficits. For some, the trauma of the death of a loved one necessitated medication to balance the careening biochemicals of the nervous system. Michelle found it helpful to choose both medication and therapy.

Feelings, once predictable and controllable, now have a stop-start of their own, which can be very frightening to the griever. This out-of-control experience may evoke additional anxiety and fear.

ANXIETY AND FEAR

Grievers relate feeling jitters, butterflies in the stomach, nameless fear, panic, and muscle tension, all manifestations of anxiety, which frequently is an undefined dread, a feeling of foreboding more general than specific. A person may be unable to place the source of the anxiety or even to recognize it as part of grieving.

Within the core of anxiety are several fears: fear of the unknown and unfamiliar, fear of being unable to cope, fear of always feeling this way, fear of being vulnerable, fear of losing another loved one, and fear of facing a new day without the one who has died. Furthermore, mourners fear losing control over themselves. The anxiety generated by that fear can be overwhelming. Control over the self seems like the only thing a griever can count on when all else is random chaos.

> . . . mourners fear losing control over themselves.

| Impact | Chaos | Adaptation | Equilibrium | Transformation |

Michelle felt "anxious every morning. I would slowly awaken and then reality hit. I got this sick feeling in the pit of my stomach and my chest. It felt so much like fear. I would try to get up and get busy to distract myself, but I felt so restless that I couldn't accomplish very much. I had to use mild medication for a while to get my fear hormones under control. I was then able to use self-talk, exercise, baking, meditation, and other positive methods to pull myself out of it.

"Once I was aware of what was happening, I could tell myself that I could handle it and it would soon pass, at least for that day. Gradually these tools led me into a calmer state."

Self-talk, meditation, exercise and, most of all, awareness help the griever through feelings of anxiety. Talking to a supportive listener is another effective strategy.

Although many grievers report sensations of anxiety, for some, paradoxically, there may be an absence of anxiety.

Martina, whose only two children died, one of a brain tumor and one by suicide, feels "less anxious than at any time in my life. I was always uptight worrying about the children. I worried that harm might come to them. Isn't it ironic that now that they are dead, I have nothing more to be anxious about? Nothing, EVER, in my life could happen that could be worse."

Martina believes that when your worst fear comes true, there is not much more to be anxious or fearful about. Many bereaved parents, now childless, may understand this sentiment. Other grievers become, conversely, hypervigilant about their loved ones. They live with awareness of life's unpredictable circumstances.

Julian, whose brother was killed in a skiing accident, says, "Because the unexpected happened, I am aware that people,

| Impact | Chaos | Adaptation | Equilibrium | Transformation |

my brother, and after that my father, can be here one moment and gone the next. So sometimes I fear that other people I love will leave or die. It makes me appreciate them and not take them for granted."

Julian articulates one of the most common threads running through the experiences of the Phoenix Grievers: daring to love again and putting themselves at risk. Ever mindful of the fact that life can be taken away at any time, they continue to love, with awareness, appreciation, and gratitude.

POWERLESSNESS

Death comes no matter how intense our efforts to prevent it. The sense of frustration and powerlessness can catch the griever unprepared. Parents, expectably, feel a particular sense of failure connected to mandates to protect their children.

Ralph, father of "Tiger," who was murdered, expresses fierce feelings of powerlessness. "I couldn't prevent his murder. I failed, as a man, as the guardian of my family, and as a father. It devastated me."

Michelle, whose daughter died of cancer, says, "I realized I was powerless to protect my child. Marie got sick and I couldn't do a thing to get her better. I believed that my role as a mother was to nurture and keep her safe, and I couldn't."

Joyce, whose daughter committed suicide, says, "Mary's death was a huge lesson in powerlessness. It was proof that I was not in control and had never been in control."

Grievers cope with these feelings in different ways. Setting a time limit for indulging these emotions, realistic self-talk, crying, yelling, exercise, meditation, yoga, and talking

| Impact | Chaos | Adaptation | Equilibrium | Transformation |

it out with supportive others are some of the ways the Phoenix Grievers have handled powerlessness and frustration. In this way they were able to discharge powerful emotions that côuld have contributed to feelings of guilt.

GUILT

During the Chaos phase, guilt appears, disconcertingly. Guilt is one of the most difficult of all human emotions to cope with. It is also one of the building blocks of the conscience. As human beings we struggle to find a balance between too much and too little, between using it as a tool and using it as a weapon. We're always trying to get it right.

We often form unrealistic expectations of ourselves, especially in regard to our loved ones. We may hold ourselves responsible for events over which we have no control, especially when we replay the sequence leading up to the death in search of an action that might have prevented it. The guilt we feel from failing to meet our high expectations may intensify when the finality of death precludes the possibility of "doing it better next time," in one mourner's words.

Joyce tormented herself with irrational guilt long after her daughter and husband had died. With intense grief work, she came to realize that "I simply did not have the power to have intervened or prevented their deaths. I know that if love could have saved either of them, they would not have died."

Love is not enough to shelter our loved ones from harm. It is one of life's disillusionments that love does not have the magical power to prevent the death of a loved one. It takes awareness and self-discipline to stop self-recrimination over events that are beyond our control.

| Impact | Chaos | Adaptation | Equilibrium | Transformation |

Julian suffered severe guilt after his brother died. His inability to prevent the death, coupled with his own survivor guilt for returning home alive, tortured his thoughts and emotions. He says, "Eventually, I had to put a stop to this torment if I were to begin to live. I learned to distinguish what I was really responsible for from what was outside of my control. I then took charge over my own life."

Guilt can torment us ruthlessly with unrealistic, perfectionist standards and rules. We may feel that we have fallen short of a perfect code of behavior, but the quest for perfection only sets us up for more guilt. On the other hand, it also enables us to evaluate our thoughts and deeds from a moral perspective. During grief, we need to discern its use or abuse.

Our very nature as human beings predisposes us to imperfect relationships. Nowhere is this more evident than when we review our relationship with the person who has died. During the process of grief, we can judge ourselves with unrelenting cruelty when evaluating what we "should" have done or said to our loved one.

In situations where the loved one has been dying over a long period of time, additional variables arise. Often, grievers will experience ambivalence when their loved one dies because their own weariness triggers feelings of relief, both for the deceased and for themselves. Widely contradictory feelings are a part of grief for many mourners. Long, debilitating illnesses are exhausting for both the patient and the family and can predispose one to feelings of intense guilt because of what are actually normal reactions to exhaustion and frustration.

Bernadette was the only caregiver for her father, who succumbed one year after suffering a stroke which had left him

| Impact | Chaos | Adaptation | Equilibrium | Transformation |

bedridden. "I didn't want him to die, and yet I knew he was suffering and so was I. I knew I couldn't do this much longer and I felt guilty for the deep relief I felt when he died. I was free from the prison of caretaking and he was free from the prison of his own body. I miss him so much that I feel crazy to have these feelings."

The finality of death impresses on us the realization that we will never have another chance to rectify past wrongs. We can use this knowledge for self-punishment or self-motivation. In judging ourselves it is important to remember that relationships are not static. They have peaks and valleys, estrangements and periods of intense bonding. The dance of relationships is one of emotional distancing and emotional attachment. All too often there is unfinished business between the griever and the deceased. There are words not spoken or spoken harshly, thoughts not revealed, actions not taken, and love not demonstrated. These human frailties constitute some of the building blocks of guilt. The search for resolution in relationships after a loved one's death is a formidable task, requiring creativity and determination.

> . . . we will never have another chance to rectify past wrongs. We can use this knowledge for self-punishment or self-motivation.

David, whose daughter Ruth was murdered, had been caught in the middle of the normally confusing pubescent years of her development, when a daughter needs to express her separateness from her parents. David felt that he didn't understand his daughter and this was one of his greatest regrets.

He says: "This is why, when I look into the eyes of the young convicts I work with, I see my daughter and her potential. I am

| Impact | Chaos | Adaptation | Equilibrium | Transformation |

able to give to them what I did not know how to give to my daughter: unconditional tolerance, understanding, and compassion. In this way I have been able to complete my unfinished business with Ruth, and in the process, by acting in her memory, I contribute to the significance of her short life."

Scott was 17 when his father committed suicide. "I was at that age where I was always disagreeing and arguing with him. I never got a chance to settle anything. I was always so angry at him for the way he lived his life. Why did he die when things between us were so unsettled?

"I searched for ways to heal the rift between us, even though he was not here. I spent a lot of time 'discussing' our relationship at his graveside. This started me on my way to forgiving him and myself for our damaged bond."

There are many situations in which there may be genuine guilt involved, situations whereby one person is directly or indirectly responsible for another's death. These events are all the more difficult and challenging for a griever searching for a means of atonement. There will be more on creative atonement in Chapter 8.

Many unrealized expectations of ourselves surface when we have come to face the uncontrollable events leading to the death of one we love. Failure, frustration, powerlessness, and guilt are all products of grief and need to be resolved. The resolution and healing of these emotions may or may not take place in the phase where it originates or feels the most intense. This process takes place gradually over the five phases of grieving. It is important for grievers to realize that the emotion of guilt offers an opportunity to evaluate thoughts and behaviors and to use the knowledge for enlightenment and growth. Another emotion of grief—anger—offers its own set of challenges and opportunities.

| Impact | Chaos | Adaptation | Equilibrium | Transformation |

ANGER

This uncomfortable emotion rears its ugly head at this time, expressing the injustice we feel. We have been victimized! Someone has been taken from us ("How could this have happened to me and how could this have happened to my child? It is so horribly unfair."). Our anger, like an arrow, seeks a target. We need to place blame for this outrage, be it on doctors, clergy, God, even the deceased, whether or not the accusations are justified. Those closest to the bereaved are often the recipients of overflowing fury.

> Our anger, like an arrow, seeks a target.

Michelle's anger "went deep. It smoldered beneath the surface of my being just waiting for a chance to escape. I searched for someone or something to blame for the tragedy. I often took it out on my family. They were a convenient target. I became irritable and crabby, causing my self-image to shrink. I was not nice and felt nasty. It took time for this distortion to improve.

"I consciously set out to cope with the anger and other emotions by understanding, acknowledging, feeling, and safely expressing them.

"I wrote in a journal to understand what was going on with me. I discharged the powerful emotions by crying, screaming, exercising, and/or talking it out with my most trusted family members, my therapist, and friends."

The sequence for successful handling of uncomfortable emotions for Michelle and others is emotional *awareness*, emotional *acceptance*, emotional *tolerance*, and emotional *expression*. Michelle called upon successive techniques used effectively by other Phoenix Grievers.

Impact	Chaos	Adaptation	Equilibrium	Transformation

Often, anger is directed at a scapegoat—perhaps medical or funeral personnel, the church, or even God—either for causing the tragedy or for failing to prevent it. It is understandable how the loss of a loved one may generate anger toward a deity.

Dianna, whose daughter was diagnosed with leukemia during her pregnancy, remembers: "I punished God by not praying for a year. Foolish, I know, but then it was over and the anger was gone . . . completely."

Many believe that doing something, anything, to discharge the pressure of anger helps as long as it harms no one. Contrary to what many of us were taught, a healthy expression of anger is part of adapting to the death of someone we love.

Elizabeth, whose daughter, granddaughter, and son-in-law were killed in a car–train collision, recalls: "For a long time I felt that the anger was controlling me, but also I believe it is what kept and keeps me going. I'm learning how to redirect the destructiveness of it. I'm beginning to take much better care of myself by first recognizing what keeps me in balance and then putting a plan into action. I have the energy from my anger, and soon I'll have just plain old energy."

Some of us are intimidated by expressions of wrath. We have learned that it is not nice to be angry. Many believe it is better to ignore it or hold it in. But anger is a natural, human response to injury. It is an emotion of survival. Expressing anger is necessary for the well being of mind and body, and suppressing it is physically dangerous. Obscuring anger is equivalent to disregarding the buildup of toxins in the body.

> Anger . . . is an emotion of survival.

| Impact | Chaos | Adaptation | Equilibrium | Transformation |

Hope, whose son Eric committed suicide, relates her experience with anger: "Expressing the painful emotion of anger was incredibly chaotic for me. For months, I held it in, hoping it would go away, but it didn't . . . it escaped. After being contained for so long, it was explosive and violent. It scared me. I sought support from my sister, my therapist, and those I considered my true friends. They did not judge me and they listened. It helped."

Gary, whose wife and daughter were killed, was overcome with waves of anger that "threatened to consume me. I couldn't stand the pressure, so I eased it by drinking. A few beers at those times soothed the 'beast.' Well, you can guess that it became out of control and there were more beers than there were reasons. I looked at myself in the rear-view mirror of my car one fine morning and saw a bleary-eyed, old, worn-out man. All I could think of was that I was letting Kim and Sarah down again. How disappointed and repulsed Kim would be if she saw me now. I felt ashamed.

"That was one of those moments in time when you feel something inside of you shift, like tumblers in a lock. I stopped drinking, started exercising (running), got the dogs, and later signed on to Big Brothers. It felt so good. I was beginning to like myself and knew that my 'angels in heaven,' Kim and Sarah, would too."

Anger is one of the most powerful tools for adaptation and change. It provides fuel for a grieving body and mind to get through the journey of grief. Like fuel, it can be used as an instrument of destruction or construction. The key is to find the vehicle of expression that contributes to growth and transformation.

Ralph's anger threatened to consume him after the murder of his son. He explains: "I could have and probably would have

| Impact | Chaos | Adaptation | Equilibrium | Transformation |

killed the men who murdered my son had I come into contact with them. The rage I experienced was a terrible, monstrous thing. I didn't know how to handle it. I only knew that I could not cause another tragedy within my family. One evening, I attended a non-specific bereavement group but was turned off when they told me that anger wasn't something they dealt with. I must have scared them with my intensity. I walked out of there and walked onto a path that changed my focus.

"I gathered together parents of murdered children. I felt that only those who had experienced what I had could understand the pain and the ferocity of rage. It worked for me and for many others. It's eleven years now and the meetings continue. What began as a way to help me and my family developed into a commitment to guide and comfort others."

When Ralph failed to find what he needed, his rage fueled the creation of something of value, for himself and others.

DEPRESSION

After experiencing the storm of emotions, the griever is exhausted and depressed. The reality of the loss spawns feelings of hopelessness. Depression appears and assumes several forms, including speeding up or slowing down of thoughts, emotions, and behaviors. It produces a cluster of symptoms, among them disturbances of sleep, appetite, self-concept, motivation, enthusiasm, and life direction. Depression is much more complex than a feeling of sadness or melancholy. Grievers find themselves feeling, acting, and behaving in ways they hadn't experienced before.

> Depression is much more complex than a feeling of sadness or melancholy.

| Impact | Chaos | Adaptation | Equilibrium | Transformation |

Barbara, the widow, remembers: "I was restless and couldn't stay still. Yet I was exhausted but unable to rest. When I stopped, the feelings of despair would overtake me. I ran away from the pain and sadness. I stayed away from home. I went to friends' homes, parties, and activities, or haunted the malls until I ran out of steam. Finally, I crashed and crashed big time.

"The time came when I couldn't even force myself out of bed. I couldn't eat. I cried continuously. I withdrew from everything and everyone. My friends forced me to go to the doctor. He said I was in a full-blown depression. It took medication and therapy to get me back to a functioning human being. I should have faced the pain in the beginning."

Disconsolate grievers will often go to any length to avoid facing their sorrow. Some will drink or self-medicate. Others may withdraw, even take to their beds until someone or something intervenes. Fumbling through the bleakness of depression does not foster healing. Consulting health professionals, who may prescribe appropriate medication along with such other therapies as individual counseling, professional support groups, or self-help groups, are more productive strategies.

Ralph, whose son was murdered, offers these suggestions: "First of all remember, if you can make it to the horizon, it [depression] suddenly breaks. Run, don't walk, to any support group that you can find. Do not, I emphasize this, withdraw into yourself. Find others who can share your experience and understand what it is to go through. Yell, scream, cry, swear, anything to get it out. Don't apologize for this. Ask God "What the hell are you doing?" Do not make a habit of taking anything that will alleviate your pain. Go straight for it and straight into it. This is the way to heal.

| Impact | Chaos | Adaptation | Equilibrium | Transformation |

"I have found that helping others helped me. I walked with them. It taught me patience and tolerance and I learned how to give a person the benefit of the doubt before I passed judgment. I believe it is a sincere privilege to have had the trust of others placed in me."

Ralph has forced his depression outward. He has reached through the black fog to extend his hands to others in need. His strong, compassionate role modeling has brought hope to those in despair. Many Phoenix Grievers have found comfort and healing through helping others in their struggles with grief. This is one of the strongest threads that these exceptional mourners have in common.

Emotional pain is a poisonous substance. The longer it is held in, the greater the potential for damage. It must be vented. Walking, talking, sharing, crying, screaming will soften the severity of the depression. What is most strongly encouraged by those who have been there is for mourners to surround themselves with supportive environments: support groups, family, friends, or people with whom they have something in common.

Maggie, whose husband died after a lengthy illness, says: "The waves of emotion would crash over me like a violent storm. I learned how to cope with grief's force. I wrote and cried and talked and surrounded myself with loving people. And so I learned that you can't stop the waves but you can learn to surf."

> "You can't stop the waves but you can learn to surf."

Occasionally, when the symptoms of sadness, hopelessness, and despondency last too long and are too intense, depression

| Impact | Chaos | Adaptation | Equilibrium | Transformation |

from grief will evolve into a clinical depression. The hopelessness turns into seemingly irreversible despair. The griever is
unable to snap out of it alone and may feel suicidal. Professional help is mandatory! The mourner may be unable to
evaluate his own depression objectively. Family, friends, and
co-workers may realize first that something is wrong.

Sarah was a junior in college when her father died suddenly.
He was all she had. Her mother had died eight years before.
"For a few months, I did okay. I went to classes, took exams,
and did well. Then, around the holidays, I began to act weird.
My friends were the first to notice.

"I slept 14–16 hours a day, and lost 15 pounds. I wore my
dad's bathrobe most of the time. I felt dead inside. My friends
were freaking out but couldn't get me to seek help. So they
brought the school nurse to me, and she was the one who saved
my life. I don't know what would have happened to me because
I was too depressed to have insight into my condition. With some
short-term medication and therapy along with a support group, I
turned my life around.

"I knew I had to make my mom and dad proud of me. It's
five years since then and I'm really healthy and fulfilled in all
areas of my life. It's what they would have wanted."

Depression is to be expected after the death of someone
beloved. The severity can range from mild to incapacitating.
It behooves the griever to be knowledgeable about the
symptoms of grief's depression and clinical depression. It
helps to be as aware as possible of the existence or worsening of any of them. The classification of symptoms of depression (Table 5–1) describes the continuum of severity of
symptoms.

| Impact | Chaos | Adaptation | Equilibrium | Transformation |

According to psychiatrist M. Rachid Och (personal communication 1998),

> If mild to moderate symptoms last more than two months or if their intensity does not diminish, then it is time to go for professional help. If there are suicidal thoughts accompanied by thoughts of acting on them, then getting help is critical! There is another phenomenon which occurs during grief and that is when people have fleeting sensory sensations connected with their loved one, such as: feeling their presence, seeing or hearing them, sensing their smell. These are normal to grief but if they persist for several months or if they increase in frequency, then getting help is imperative.

The Phoenix Grievers encourage mourners to be vigilant about their moods. If there is concern about emotional stability, the mourner should see a doctor as soon as possible and seek out a supportive environment, be it with friends, family members, a therapist, a group, or all of the above. Medication may be indicated for a brief interval when a depression seriously interferes with a person's day-to-day functioning and diminishes his motivation for living. Ratey and Johnson (1997) report that when the newly widowed received treatment in the form of counseling or medication, the risks of developing serious clinical depression fell from 50 percent to as low as 10 percent.

Table 5–1. Continuum of Depression Symptoms

Mild	Moderate	Severe
Sorrow	Deep sadness	Prolonged feelings of hopelessness
Mild crying spells	Severe crying spells	May be no crying spells
Irritability and anger	Episodes of rage	May have absence of emotion

Impact	Chaos	Adaptation	Equilibrium	Transformation

Mild	Moderate	Severe
Brief periods of insomnia	Chronic insomnia or feeling unrefreshed by sleep	Severe sleep disturbances
Mild loss of appetite/weight	Suppressed or increased appetite; weight gain or loss of 10 pounds	Not caring about eating or compulsive overeating
Apathy, mild anxiety, loss of enthusiasm	Panic attacks; inability to tolerate being alone for long periods or withdrawal	Feelings of worthlessness Complete withdrawal from people
Mild preoccupation and/or inability to concentrate	Moderate periods of memory loss and preoccupation	Lack of personal hygiene
	Frequent guilt feelings	Obsessive guilt
Fleeting thoughts of death	Preoccupation with morbid thoughts	Giving away possessions
	Somatizations	Putting affairs in order
		Suicidal thoughts and plan
		Psychotic thinking
		Somatic delusions

- **Mild** symptoms may or may not need professional intervention. They may respond to self-help techniques and a support network.
- **Moderate** symptoms require a consultation with the family physician and/or mental health specialist.
- **Severe** symptoms necessitate immediate medical and/or psychiatric intervention.

Note: All symptoms should be considered serious if there is alcohol and/or drug use and/or if there is suicidal thinking, especially if there are specific plans with available means and/or psychotic thinking present.

| Impact | Chaos | Adaptation | Equilibrium | Transformation |

Often, it is a griever's therapist who detects a more serious depression and makes the appropriate referral for a medical opinion. Since all medications carry some side effects, the
medication issue is one of risk vs. benefit. Qualified professionals know that the griever will not experience this depression forever, and that with the proper intervention, it will
eventually subside.

ALIENATION

Grievers may sense a disconnection, a kind of barrier between
themselves and others. Their feelings of alienation may precipitate their withdrawal from people. Generally, a brief period of retreat allows them time to draw inward, to absorb
the grief, and to protect themselves from too much sensory
bombardment. Sometimes, because
the death of a loved one alters the perception of being the same as everyone
else, of belonging, grievers may become angry and disappointed with
non-grievers. "They can't understand
what I'm going through," says one
young widow who feels different, changed somehow. "I'm no
longer marching in the same parade," says a grieving father.

> . . . the death of a loved one alters the perception of being the same as everyone else, of belonging. . . .

Joyce reflects about feelings of alienation. "I wish I had known
about the isolation resulting from this kind of emotional pain. I
felt so alone for such a long time. None of my well-meaning
friends could break through. I was totally disconnected until I
found other mothers who had suffered this same loss and could
truly understand."

Dianna, whose daughter Grace died of leukemia, says, "It
was a mistake to isolate myself. The healing could not proceed.

Impact	Chaos	Adaptation	Equilibrium	Transformation

I came out of my isolation on a vacation trip, of all things. I met other people who were going through personal anguish. Reaching out to them and finding a common ground was extremely beneficial for all of us. It became a vital tool for the healing process to go forward. At that time, my life was changed forever, and to this day, I still go back to that beautiful place."

Phoenix Grievers are unanimous in finding that reaching out, whether to help others or for themselves, is a key to healing. Many mourners are helped by support groups. Those who believe they are singular in their grief feel reassured to find others who have experienced similar losses. They find that a common language makes them feel understood and connected. Receiving and giving support to others who grieve is therapeutic for all concerned. Bear in mind, however, that what is comforting for some may not comfort others. At no other time is the uniqueness of each individual more evident than in the aftermath of losing a loved one.

> Those who believe they are singular in their grief feel reassured to find others who have experienced similar losses.

GRIEF WORK

The primary purpose of the Chaos phase is to be aware of, acknowledge, and safely express the painful emotions caused by the death of a loved one. As the mind and body absorb the reality of the death, the griever responds with emotions such as anger, rage, guilt, blame, depression, inconsolable sorrow, anxiety, and fear. The griever needs to release the intense and painful emotions of grief in a safe, supported, and secure manner.

Discharging pent-up emotions can be difficult. We may be restricted by the fear of losing control over ourselves or the

| Impact | Chaos | Adaptation | Equilibrium | Transformation |

fear of what others may think. It takes creativity and determination to overcome these feelings but the effort is well worth it. The expression of emotional distress is constructive; it moves the griever forward on the continuum of grief.

When the force of these emotions is overpowering and/or can't find a means of expression, grievers need assistance and guidance. They need others on their team to help them stabilize the turbulence and cope with their emotions. It should be remembered that reaching out is not easy during this phase because grievers are wounded and exhausted. The challenge is to reach out for support despite the chaos raging internally.

FOR THE GRIEVER

Phoenix Grievers recommend the following:

- Continue nurturing your baseline needs.
- Be aware of the normal feelings of grief. Knowledge is power.
- Acknowledge and accept what you are feeling.
- Find support to safely express your emotions.
- Use *reflective* and *expressive* techniques:

Reflective:	*Expressive*:
meditation	crying, screaming, sobbing, singing
journal recording (written or audio)	talking with others
music	hitting pillows
yoga	hitting/kicking a punching bag
self-talk (calming and encouraging)	walking, running, physical activities, housework, etc.

Impact	Chaos	Adaptation	Equilibrium	Transformation

- Gather a support team: family, friends, clergy, therapist and/or group.
- Search for role models who have been through your specific loss situation.
- Keep it simple; eliminate anything unnecessary from daily life.
- Recognize that this pain will not last forever. This too shall pass.
- Never let go of hope.

FOR THE THERAPIST

The therapist is in a key position to inform, guide and support grievers through the Phase of Chaos when emotions erupt with a ferocity. Therapists might consider using a variation of the crisis model of intervention, which includes assessing the client, identifying risks, co-creating a plan and establishing a support team.

The therapist should quickly explore the mourner's past coping mechanisms for dealing with crises or stressful situations and should encourage connection to supportive others. As a plan is developed to provide a modicum of safety, structure, and connectedness, the griever should feel secure enough to express the painful emotions of his or her loss.

The plan should include restoration of physiological homeostasis, since very little will be accomplished if the griever has not been eating, sleeping, or establishing some structure in a chaotic internal and external environment. The plan includes stabilization of emotional turbulence to minimize the anxiety and fear the mourner is feeling and should be in place during the first session.

Transported to a new world, the griever is not familiar with the protocols for survival and is in need of guidance, support,

| Impact | Chaos | Adaptation | Equilibrium | Transformation |

and direction in this time of disorientation. Accordingly, the therapist's role is an active one during the first three phases of grief.

Monitoring for untoward complications must be included in the therapeutic model. Clinical depression, panic attacks, suicidality, even homicidality may surface and, of course, demand additional treatment modalities. The griever's feelings of profound detachment and alienation will be assuaged by connecting to others who comprise the griever's team. The therapist should guide the griever toward developing a supportive network, thus laying the foundation for the beginning of the next phase, Adaptation.

Table 5–2. The Phoenix Model of Grief: Chaos Phase

Needs	Tasks	Intervention
For:	*To:*	*Use:*
Food, shelter, rest, sleep	Maintain physiological stability	Crisis intervention and brief focused therapy to control emotional and environmental turbulence
Safety and security	Seek security and safety measures	
	Acknowledge, accept, and express the emotions of grief	Humanistic model
		More direct approach (griever is confused and uncertain)
Preparatory belonging	Connect with others; resist isolation	Guide toward community resources (professional and non-professional) for support and advice

Impact	Chaos	Adaptation	Equilibrium	Transformation

The Phoenix Model's Chaos phase integrates the physiological, safety/security, and belonging needs described by Maslow. Crisis intervention combined with a supportive, humanistic approach will facilitate the griever's progress during this phase. The introduction of a more directive, interactive modality (brief, solution-focused therapy and/or cognitive-behavioral therapy) will assist the griever in achieving some control. The structured techniques should focus on coping with the altered environment through problem solving while supporting emotional expression of the pain of loss.

Therapists should:

- **Listen:** The griever will let you know his level of functioning and coping.
- **Normalize:** The griever needs to know that this intense, crazy time is normal in the acute phase of grief.
- **Assess:** Identify the needs and tasks of this phase according to the Phoenix Model.
- **Plan:** Together with the griever, design corrective measures for deficiency areas.
- **Intervene:** Decide on a time frame for implementation of realistic short-term goals. Think small.
- **Support:** The griever's efforts at emotional expression and physiological homeostasis need encouragement.
- **Educate:** Continue to reinforce the elements of the grief process. Hand out a copy of the Phoenix Model of Grief. Grievers have difficulty concentrating and may refer to it later.
- **Monitor:** Be alert for signs and symptoms of worsening emotional distress requiring additional intervention, such as medication, hospitalization, family therapy, or group support. Make the appropriate referral.

| Impact | Chaos | Adaptation | Equilibrium | Transformation |

SUMMARY

- The phase of Chaos is a time of confusion, depression, anxiety, and fear.
- Grief's emotional sequelae surface and their healthy discharge constitutes the grief work for this phase.
- Awareness, acknowledgment, tolerance, and permission to express symptoms advance the griever along the grief process.

A villager told the grievers that the horse in the corner of the corral ignored a past injury and continued to run as if nothing had happened. He is now lame.

The villager pointed to a lively horse that was running and prancing about. This one also had been injured but had reacted to the pain and taken the time to heal. The little group contemplated the meaning of this and they moved on. . . .

| Impact | Chaos | Adaptation | Equilibrium | Transformation |

6

Further Challenges: Phase Two—Chaos (continued)

And it came to pass that strange maladies overcame the grievers and they were afraid. One spoke of an "invisible knife in her heart," another of a mysterious "lump in his throat" through which food would not pass, yet another of a "malaise of the body."

And the guides spoke: "These too are the signs of grief."

In the preceding chapter, we examined some of grief's emotional manifestations in the Chaos phase. This chapter addresses the body's response to the loss of a loved one. There is a saying that the body believes everything we think and grief produces some powerful thoughts. These thoughts in turn produce feelings so intense that they register as physical pain in the body. As one young widow stated, "I could feel a pain in my heart as real as if I had open-heart surgery." The mind grieves and so does the body.

The symptoms expressed by the body are often an exquisite directive alerting the griever to the presence of an invisible internal wound. This injury needs attention. Proactive measures should be established as quickly as possible after

| Impact | Chaos | Adaptation | Equilibrium | Transformation |

the loss of a loved one lest the unattended physiological imbalances caused by grief precipitate more problems in their own right.

THE BODY GRIEVES

Phase Two
Chaos
The Body Grieves
Sleep
Appetite
Sex
Grief and Physical Illness
Grief and Mental Illness
Grief and Death

Grief is a full-time job. Time and energy must be redirected from some other focus and devoted to its healthy resolution. Grievers need rest, sleep, nutrition, and an organized routine. The physical effects of the grief process are exhausting and potentially debilitating. When grief is piled on top of other responsibilities, burnout ensues, and the odds of contracting an illness rise.

Many physical symptoms of grief appear during the Chaos phase. Headaches, stomachaches, and other ailments may surface or intensify. As James (1988) observes: "It [grief] has all the physical symptoms of stress and illness: exhaustion, shortness of breath, inability to eat or sleep; your throat tightens, your face aches, your eyes are swollen, your head hurts, your whole body aches, and it seems that it will last forever" (p. 81).

These are discouraging words for a griever to hear and it is important to realize that it *does not last forever*. Furthermore, when one is made aware of the physical symptoms of grief, one can prepare for handling them in a constructive way. As with all crisis situations, awareness and proactive responses will help to avoid complications.

Several changes occur in bodily functions. Appetite, sleep, and sexual habits may increase or decrease. These changes

| Impact | Chaos | Adaptation | Equilibrium | Transformation |

can be alarming if grievers are unaware of their normality at this time. Grief's effects on these drives interrupt the natural rhythm of our bodies. Since these needs contribute to the maintenance and pleasure aspects of our lives, these disruptions can be serious.

Another disconcerting phenomenon of grief is the eruption of symptoms that imitate the cause of death of the loved one.

Lorna, whose 40-year-old husband suffered a fatal heart attack, became frightened when she developed severe chest pain. She even drove herself to the emergency room one night, only to be reassured that she was all right. Unconvinced, she went to her physician the next day.

She recalls: "I believed I was having a heart attack and no one was taking me seriously. I needed someone to tell me I was okay. The doctor put me on some mild medicine for anxiety and my symptoms began to subside. When my therapist made the connection between Mike's heart attack and my symptoms, I felt relieved. This I could understand."

Another young woman, whose mother died of a brain aneurysm, developed excruciating migraine headaches. It took years of medical intervention before she sought the help of a therapist. She learned that denying her grief over the death of her mother was having a physical effect on her body. The headaches were emblematic of her mother's brain aneurysm. They gradually decreased as she was able to fully mourn her loss.

Be cautioned that no symptom should be taken lightly. All require a physician's evaluation, which is something that should be sought early in bereavement. Grief renders us vulnerable to illness and the primary care physician is in a pivotal position to evaluate, monitor, and possibly treat the griever. She becomes part of the team.

| Impact | Chaos | Adaptation | Equilibrium | Transformation |

SLEEP

There are several ways that grief affects sleeping patterns. Individuals may have difficulty falling asleep or staying asleep, or they may experience restless, interrupted sleep, early morning awakening, or excessive sleep. Grievers may dread upsetting dreams or nightmares and may be afraid to sleep. Whatever the disturbance, a sleep deficiency compromises a griever's functioning.

Noella had to meet her obligations to her children after Bob died. However, she could not bring herself to go to sleep in the bed she had shared for so many years with her husband. "I knew that I had to sleep, but couldn't bear to be in that lonely bed. For two years, I fell asleep on the couch and that was the only way I could do it. It worked for me. I don't even remember when I returned to my bed, it just happened."

Grievers do what it takes to try to get some sleep, but, like any other biological drive, the way some choose to meet their needs might not be healthy. Several have reported long periods of time using drugs or alcohol to help them sleep. Although short periods of medication may help, long dependencies do not. They may even alter the natural course of grief. Running away into substance dependence or excessive activity is not helpful, nor is pretending nothing has happened.

Paradoxically, healthy life habits may be established during the mourning phases because grief presents new choices.

Julian, whose brother Vince died in a skiing accident, "wasn't sleeping. I had disturbing dreams and whatever sleep I had was very restless. I didn't want to take drugs so I chose the outdoors instead. It was a big help for me, being outside and taking up mountain biking. I got to exercise, hang around with upbeat

| Impact | Chaos | Adaptation | Equilibrium | Transformation |

people, and I began to sleep well. It gave me the double benefit of improving my health and tiring myself out enough to sleep at night and awaken refreshed."

A gentle and moderate management of insomnia symptoms is encouraged. The Phoenix Grievers' suggestions for the physical manifestations of grief are included later in this chapter.

APPETITE

This complex drive is under siege during the grieving process. Its normal function is to nourish and sustain the body. Now it reacts to the stresses of grief. For many mourners, providing fuel for the body's engine becomes a secondary motive for eating. The primary incentive may be easing the emotions of anxiety, depression, loneliness, and fear. These alterations in appetite can affect the body, mind, and self-esteem.

Martina, whose two children had died, felt the "grief regulating my appetite. It was as though someone, not myself, had control over the master switch. For weeks, I could barely eat anything and I lost a lot of weight. My friends were beginning to get very concerned. I didn't want to eat, I didn't care.

"One day I woke up and I was hungry. I don't know how this happened, but it wasn't good. Now, I couldn't eat enough. It soothed the pain inside. I ate and ate. Soon, I was a blimp. I found myself in a worse mess than before. My self-esteem was deeply affected."

Many grievers can relate to Martina's description. The checks and balances of our appestat go awry. Mourners find it helpful to stabilize the appetite as quickly as possible to

| Impact | Chaos | Adaptation | Equilibrium | Transformation |

ensure adequate strength through the work of grieving. A Phoenix Griever reports: "I set regular times to eat small meals. I forced myself into a pattern and tempted myself with favorite foods. I knew it was one small step toward healing and I had to take it."

Surviving on junk food, is a no-no according to many grievers. Maintaining adequate nutrition through sensible eating helps to stabilize an out-of-control body. A grieving father offers the following analogy: "Your car wouldn't get very far if it had no gas or if you put in cheap, tainted gasoline. How do you expect your body to run under the same circumstances?"

Taking care of yourself when you least care about yourself is imperative. The body that will transport you through this world is your "space suit" for traversing the planet. It needs to be adequately maintained, and that takes courage.

SEX

You can be sure that an area so contentious in life will be a candidate for conflict during grieving. Add the factor that the libidinal needs of men and women may be different during grief and you have a situation that can distance or alienate a couple from each other when they need each other most.

In the midst of her grief, Michelle "felt less like making love than ever before in my life. I felt guilty for even considering it. Yet, I knew it brought comfort to Mark. Even though my desire was at a sub-zero level, I wanted to do something for him. And it helped me to know that I had soothed his pain, even for a brief time."

Michelle is a sensitive woman who was fully aware that she and Mark differed in their sexual needs during grief. As

| Impact | Chaos | Adaptation | Equilibrium | Transformation |

she gave comfort to her husband she received comfort as well. Phoenix Grievers advise not to judge the needs of others during grief. Communication, compromise, and understanding are the best resources. Participate in your partner's needs if you wish as long as you are not harmed in any way.

Sexual desire may increase or decrease during grief and this is normal. However, our beliefs about sex are as colorful and varied as a kaleidoscope. If we wrap sex in guilt or define it as wrong, disgusting, selfish, or unnatural after the death of a loved one, then it will feel bad. If we perceive sex to be a natural appetite of the human body, then its expression during grief is as normal as at any other time. More important, as Raphael (1983) observes about sex and grief: "There is a need for comfort and reassurance against the pain of the loss, the rejection, and the fear of being alone" (p. 214). The mutual reaching out to comfort offers consolation for many grievers. Some would say it is life-affirming.

Jolene and Carl were grieving the death of Carl's mother, who had lived with them and who was a source of constant love, support, and assistance. Carl tended to withdraw when he felt emotional pressure, thus distancing himself from Jolene.

After a couple of weeks, Carl "woke up to the realization of what I was doing. The very person I needed to be close to and comforted by was being pushed away—by me! I felt that I would break apart if I allowed myself to be intimate. That's how fragile and vulnerable I was. I had to let her back into my space and I did. Yes, I cried and it [grief] hurt so much, but then I felt consoled and more at peace.

"Don't push your loved ones away when you're grieving. That would be a big mistake."

There are many grievers who feel the way Carl does, that sex can bridge isolation and loneliness. And there are just as

| Impact | Chaos | Adaptation | Equilibrium | Transformation |

many who feel differently, who for a long while are unable to participate in the intimacy of sex. The Phoenix Grievers advise others to be very aware of and sensitive to their own and their partner's needs.

Awareness is a difficult achievement during grief, but it is extremely empowering. Phoenix Grievers like Michelle and Carl were aware of what was happening to them. Although Michelle's libido had plummeted, she was mindful of Mark's need and was able to comfort him. Carl was conscious of pulling away from his partner and pushed himself back, thus reversing his tendency toward detachment. In these situations, the bond of intimacy was maintained.

GRIEF AND PHYSICAL ILLNESS

Anything that upsets the exquisite balance of the body creates an imbalance in the mind and spirit as well. The stress of grief can compromise the immune system of the griever and precipitate physical illness.

One groundbreaking study on the cancer-mind–body connection (Simonton et al. 1978) found that psychological stress influences the hypothalamus, the limbic system, the immune system, and the endocrine system, thereby sabotaging our natural defenses against cancer. Prolonged grief is prolonged stress and thus affects the biochemistry of the body, the functioning of the mind, the range of emotions, and the vitality of the soul. Since the death of a loved one is a severe stressor, one could contend that mourners are at increased risk for the development of a malignancy. A key factor in the study was the discov-

> Prolonged grief is prolonged stress and thus affects the biochemistry of the body, the functioning of the mind, the range of emotions, and the vitality of the soul.

| Impact | Chaos | Adaptation | Equilibrium | Transformation |

ery that stress leads to prolonged feelings of depression and despair. Simonton and colleagues postulated that if depression and despair could be reversed with hope and anticipation, then cancer would not occur.

The loss of a loved one scores as the highest level of stress conceptualized by numerical indicators. The Holmes and Rahe (1967) Social Readjustment Rating Scale assigns 100 points, its highest rating, to the death of a spouse, and many people believe that the death of a child should have an even higher rating. If there are concurrent stress variables, then the score increases, heightening a griever's vulnerability to illness, even death. Raphael (1983) reports grief's implication in impaired physical health, psychosomatic disorders, psychiatric disorders, depression, even mortality. She suggests that these are only *possible* outcomes of bereavement and includes them along with the successful resolutions. It appears that grief has the power to affect positive and negative changes in the body and mind of the griever.

Richard, a 70-year-old widower, remembers "every moment of the day Martha died two years ago. Time stopped for me and I think I stopped living. Anyway, you guessed it, grief hit my body with the development of a lymphoma. It sure propelled me out of my grief.

"I began to live again. Isn't that strange? I began to eat well, golf with friends, attend activities, all while undergoing treatment for cancer! I finally dismantled the shrine I had made of my house and kept only what was meaningful.

"There is a support group for lymphoma survivors and I am the moderator. I make myself available to help others like me. Life is okay!"

Richard is a lucky man. He heeded the wake-up call before he didn't wake up at all. Many of us are the same. We

| Impact | Chaos | Adaptation | Equilibrium | Transformation |

meander through life in a half-trance, especially if we're grieving, only waking up when life itself is threatened.

Phoenix Grievers strongly urge mourners to begin to restore order and structure to their daily lives. Another consistent suggestion is to connect to others. They recommend the
formation of a support team. Consider the following experience:

Michelle called upon her therapist, priest, family physician,
parents, siblings, and support group. She was quite aware that
the stress of Marie's illness and grief after her death could take
a further toll on her. She initiated proactive measures to defend
herself and her family against this contingency.

"I was afraid not to take care of us. I refused to let anything
I could control hurt us. I focused on nutrition, sleep, rest, exercise, quiet time, and talking to my 'team.' I felt like I was gear-
ing up for a long marathon run and I would be as prepared as
possible."

Phoenix Grievers acknowledge that this is very difficult to
do because there were many moments when they just didn't
care. It is very important for other grievers to realize that
they need courage and determination to do what needs to be
done when they least feel like doing it. The long-range benefits cannot be denied. The stress hormones, adrenaline and
cortisol, mediated by the sympathetic nervous system, flood
the besieged body in an effort to restore equilibrium. The very
mechanisms of the body that mobilize to defend against one
of life's greatest assaults—grief—can, after chronic siege,
begin to alter and/or destroy cells, tissues, organs, and systems of the body. In situations involving a lengthy dying trajectory, family members may be especially prone to immuno-
logical siege.

| Impact | Chaos | Adaptation | Equilibrium | Transformation |

Cassandra was 45 when her mother, with whom she lived and whom she cared for, died. "I had no life outside of work except my devotion to my mother. She was my world. I nurtured her for so long that I lost sight of how to take care of myself. I neglected my health so badly that two years later, I was diagnosed with rheumatoid arthritis.

"I was lucky that it was a mild form and rapidly came under control. That was my wake-up call. It was time to stop recycling through painful grieving and begin living—healthily. I started a nutrition and exercise program and a stress-reduction class. Healing my own grief allowed me to help others through developing a yoga class for grievers!"

Cassandra's statement about not knowing how to take care of herself illustrates how this neglect compounds the consequences of grief. It is extremely important to try to find a support system as early as possible in order to distribute the burdens of care equitably, because the demands of grief quickly follow the long siege of losing a loved one.

GRIEF AND MENTAL ILLNESS

One of my earliest mentors was the late Dr. David Moriarty, psychiatrist and psychoanalyst. Several of his written works had to do with pathological grief. In 1967, he wrote about his clinical experiences and was convinced that "the death of a loved one often precipitates various types of disabling emotional illness in addition to depression. The kind of illness depends on the vulnerability of the premorbid personality" (pp. 15–16). He was struck by the number of psychiatric patients who had lost loved ones and attributed the appearances of many psychiatric illnesses to grief.

| Impact | Chaos | Adaptation | Equilibrium | Transformation |

Stroebe and Stroebe (1987) wrote "There is a great deal of evidence suggesting that the widowed have higher inception rates to psychiatric care than the married and that the excesses are associated most closely with recent rather than long-term bereavement" (p. 143). We may conclude that the death of a loved one is a powerful variable in precipitating mental illnesses in certain susceptible individuals. The question, of course, is why are some more vulnerable than others?

There is a category of psychosis defined in the *DSM-IV* handbook called Brief Psychotic Disorder. It can be described as a form of temporary insanity followed by an eventual full return to premorbid level of functioning. Jared's experience illustrates this viewpoint.

Jared's wife Ellen was killed when she was hit by a car while crossing the street. He was determined to put the tragedy behind him and resume his life as quickly as possible. He failed to grieve. One year later, he became engaged and his wedding was planned for the Christmas holidays. A week before the festivities, his fiancée was hit by a car and killed while crossing the street.

Jared's coping mechanisms couldn't defend him against the shock. He began hearing voices plotting against him and believed he was receiving messages from the FBI through air-conditioning vents at work. He wasn't sleeping or eating and when he barricaded himself in his office, his very concerned co-workers called the police. He was admitted to a psychiatric facility.

Very quickly, his symptoms were brought under control and he was released to undergo outpatient therapy along with medication for the next six months. He began the process of grieving each loss and subsequently had a full recovery.

| Impact | Chaos | Adaptation | Equilibrium | Transformation |

A sudden catastrophic shock can temporarily disable a person's previous coping mechanisms. Yet others respond differently. Contrast Jared's experience with that of Megan.

A sudden catastrophic shock can temporarily disable a person's previous coping mechanisms.

Megan was a young woman in her early thirties, whose husband Steven died in the first year of their marriage. Within one year, her father died. When she became engaged a few years later, Megan thought her mourning days were behind her. Within two months, her fiancé was diagnosed with cancer and died within a year.

Megan did not develop a psychosis or a clinical depression but she did experience a painful grieving process for each loved one. She gathered her support team: friends, family, physician, therapist, and God and began to heal once again.

Megan's insight is expressed in her words: "The experience of loving these wonderful human beings has made me stronger."

Megan continues to be sensitive, open, and loving. She is less harried than before, has more time to listen and empathize with others, and has an amazing ability to forgive others through understanding their viewpoint. She is a role model of strength and courage. How is it that she is able to suffer a triple blow and retain the positive elements of her personality and exhibit more growth?

The answers have as much to do with Megan's capacity to learn during grief as with the circumstances surrounding her losses. Siebert (1996) observed that "our attitudes determine our well-being more than our circumstances" (p. 8).

Stroebe and Stroebe (1987) concluded from their research that the rate of psychiatric illness was higher than that of the general population in those who had suffered sudden bereave-

| Impact | Chaos | Adaptation | Equilibrium | Transformation |

ment, as Jared did twice. However, they found that prior adult bereavement experience, such as Megan's, could in some way prepare the griever for the process. Such is the paradox of grief.

GRIEF AND DEATH

Death from grief is a multifactorial phenomenon. Unfortunately, it is romanticized in fiction, music, movies, and theater, doing considerable disservice to the griever who needs hope to continue living without the loved one. Often death from grief has its roots in the mourner's belief system. "I can't live without her," said one octogenarian who died less than twenty-four hours after his spouse. "My life is over," stated a father who succumbed to leukemia eighteen months after his only child died. The shipping magnate, Aristotle Onassis, developed myasthenia gravis with fatal results after his only son was killed. Many unexpected deaths can be attributed to unresolved grief.

Joyce and Maurice's daughter died by suicide when she was in college. Joyce believes that "when Mary killed herself, life began to constrict and diminish for Maurice. Two years later he suffered a stroke and a heart attack from which he died. It wasn't the real cause of his death. He died of a grief-related illness, a broken heart."

If we accept the cause of Maurice's death as Joyce describes it, then why was her bereavement outcome different? As described in Chapter 1, her experience points to her determination to make her own life count and make a difference in other grievers' lives. She initially withdrew for a short time, then forced herself to find role models for grieving, thereby neutralizing her sense of alienation and isolation. Thus, she

| Impact | Chaos | Adaptation | Equilibrium | Transformation |

advanced past the first and second levels of the hierarchy of needs (survival and safety/security) toward belonging through connecting with other grievers. For Joyce, the mechanisms for growth were an awareness of her unhealthy grieving, acknowledging the need for change, commitment to change, and courageously taking action.

This chapter emphasizes the critical importance of being aware of grief's power over the essential drives of the body as well as its ultimate survival. The sequelae of grief seek discharge and expression. It takes awareness and creativity to find means to expel the toxic buildup healthily. The initiation of proactive responses rather than reactive measures enhances the outcome of bereavement and may prevent grievers from becoming unnecessary victims of the deaths of their loved ones.

GRIEF WORK

The body is besieged by grief's turbulence during this time of Chaos. As with any organism under attack, the body must defend itself. This requires a knowledge and awareness of the vulnerability of the body and mind during active mourning. Mourners meet the challenges through certain tasks: the recognition, acknowledgment, and therapeutic management of symptoms, syndromes, and illnesses.

The defense begins with careful monitoring of body (including the mind) functioning, identifying deficiencies or imbalances, and restoring homeostasis. This base supports the expression of grief's emotions. The griever needs adequate food, rest, sleep, and a place of refuge. This essential prescription offers the griever the opportunity to form a solid base upon which to support future growth.

Impact	Chaos	Adaptation	Equilibrium	Transformation

FOR THE GRIEVER

Phoenix Grievers advocate the following:

- Learn what grief does to the body and mind and realize you are vulnerable.
- Encourage yourself to eat, rest, sleep, and exercise. Ask someone to check up on you.
- Monitor yourself in order to detect symptoms of change.
- Use your support team. Do not isolate yourself.
- Be sure to see your primary care physician. Follow his/her advice.
- Continue using techniques from the previous chapter.
- Set aside a time to grieve. Life's hectic pace may leave little time to feel and express grief's emotions.
- Be aware of the health of dependent grievers such as children and the elderly.
- Eliminate unnecessary obligations. Keep it simple.
- You will make it through. Never let go of hope!

FOR THE THERAPIST

The body and mind are under siege and the biochemical weapons of defense engulf the vulnerable griever. The therapist should remain aware of the principles of stress and the grieving process and apply therapeutic measures to protect the griever from harm. Reactive measures should be instituted immediately. Proactive measures should include educating the griever and designing a program for health maintenance and stress reduction.

The Phoenix Model integrates the elements of the Maslow hierarchy of needs. Since grievers plummet to the baseline of functioning, they need to be nurtured and guided. The

| Impact | Chaos | Adaptation | Equilibrium | Transformation |

physiological needs of the body take precedence, since no other forward movement will take place if the body is unable to function.

Table 6–1. The Phoenix Model of Grief: Chaos Phase
(The Body Grieves)

Needs	Tasks	Intervention
For:	*To:*	*Use:*
Food, shelter, rest, sleep	Maintain physiological stability	Crisis intervention and brief focused therapy to control emotional and environmental turbulence
Safety and security	Establish security and safety measures	
	Acknowledge, accept, and express the emotions of grief	*Humanistic model
	Understand bodily symptoms of grief and monitor health	Establish referral/ consultation network and treatment if necessary
Preliminary belonging	Connect with others; avoid isolation	Use creativity in forming support team
		Guide toward community resources for assistance, support, and advice

* The griever's emotional expression is facilitated by a warm, accepting therapist with whom a bond of trust is established.

Grievers need to feel safe during this time of Chaos, and anxiety needs to be curtailed. A structured environment, realistic plan, and supportive others will begin to relieve these needs. Additional intervention may be necessary (medication, group therapy, hospitalization).

| Impact | Chaos | Adaptation | Equilibrium | Transformation |

The needs for attachment and belonging are beginning to resurface. Grievers need the support of family, friends, and others, including professionals. The therapist should assist the griever in putting together a team for the specific situation. Be creative. Each griever will need a little different therapeutic intervention. The support team is a vital component of constructively dealing with grief, since others often provide for a large portion of the nurturing and sustenance needs of the griever.

Meeting the physiological and safety needs and protecting the body are priorities during this phase of Chaos. Bear in mind that the griever is beginning to experience the next phase of grief, Adaptation, concurrently. That is to say painful emotions, bodily sensations, and anxiety may be at an acute level while the griever is struggling to adapt to life without the lost loved one. Hence, the griever is also struggling with an altered environment.

Attending to physiological needs and the release of pent-up emotions will begin to decrease the biochemical imbalances in the body. Stress reduction methods will contribute to increasing the body's resistance to illness. A connection to a support network eliminates alienation and isolation. Grievers need others. They also need information, guidance, and support to begin to stabilize in the internal and external environments. Brief, solution-oriented, focused modalities may be appropriately introduced at this level. The following pointers should assist the helping person:

- **Listen:** Pay attention to somatic complaints. The griever will often speak in terms of somatic metaphor when relating to grieving. A "broken heart" warrants exploration, perhaps an evaluation.
- **Normalize:** Affirm that cognitive and somatic complaints are part of this period of grief.

| Impact | Chaos | Adaptation | Equilibrium | Transformation |

- **Assess:** Identify the griever's needs. Use the Phoenix Model to determine physiological, safety, security and belonging needs, and imbalances.
- **Plan:** Co-design, with the griever, proactive and/or reactive plans for this phase.
- **Intervene:** Be sure a support team is in place. Prioritize treatments.
- **Support:** Uphold the griever's suggestions for homeostasis.
- **Educate:** Continue to teach the griever about grief in a "you are here" approach (to show the griever that grief has landmarks and that there is hope).
- **Monitor:** Pay attention to your gut instinct for areas that might prove problematic. Be alert for symptoms of complications. Be prepared to make the appropriate referral, *stat.*

SUMMARY

- The body also "grieves" for the lost loved one and any of the bodily processes or functions may be affected.
- Proactive measures for maintaining health include rest, nutrition, exercise, sleep, reduction of stressors, and simplicity of routine.
- Reactive measures for treating symptoms are to be discussed and partnered with the griever's physician and any other members of the health team.
- This phase of grief needs to be handled firmly and competently as it is a critical passage toward a positive long-term outcome.

The phase of Chaos often coincides with the elementary work of the next phase, that of Adaptation. Grievers are try-

| Impact | Chaos | Adaptation | Equilibrium | Transformation |

ing to live in the world without the loved one at a time when they are in the most emotional and physical distress. They are moving albeit uncertainly, further along the journey through grief.

Before they moved on, the little group of grievers were counseled by their guides to rest for a while and give credence to their pain, confusion, and sorrow, lest they become like the crippled horse they observed in the meadow, unable to fully participate in life.

| Impact | Chaos | Adaptation | Equilibrium | Transformation |

7

Lessons and Opportunities: Phase Three—Adaptation

And it came to pass that the wearied grievers came to a cave where light could not reach. Their journey could not continue without passing through the cave. And so they entered and were plummeted into darkness. . . .

The stormy emotions and the physical challenges of the Chaos and Impact phases have left the mourner depleted. The most pressing emotional and physical demands of bereavement (making funeral arrangements, answering sympathy cards, dealing with legal or financial matters) have been addressed. The demands of grief have taken their toll. The next phase may seem like a time of hopelessness, but Adaptation is the birthplace of hope.

> Adaptation is the birthplace of hope.

Because of the depression and exhaustion, Adaptation may appear quiet on the outside but it is anything but passive. It is a lot like hibernation, a time of rest from which one emerges ready to face the growth that spring demands.

Implicit in this phase is the symbolic farewell to the old life that ended with the death of a person and the death of a

Impact	Chaos	Adaptation	Equilibrium	Transformation

lifestyle. During this time, the griever begins a pragmatic review of what has transpired, contemplating the past and confronting the present. This begins the authentic acceptance of the reality that the loved one is gone and its aftermath.

Grievers may appear to slip into a mood resembling a clinical depression, but clinical depression has a great emptiness within its nucleus. The melancholy of Adaptation contains a silent core of activity where assessment and planning are taking place. (As noted in Chapter 5, symptoms of clinical depression should always be evaluated by a professional.) The despair of grief forms a bridge from hopelessness to hope.

Toward the end of the Adaptation phase, the implications of the loss become clearer and the griever begins consciously and subconsciously to formulate a plan to cope without the loved one. This is a pivotal point of decision for the griever's future. It is a dress rehearsal for the new life.

FAREWELL TO THE OLD LIFE

Adaptation begins with the acknowledgment that the loved one is no longer physically in this world. This is less an epiphany than the cumulative effect of the many tiny events that send the unmistakable message that somebody is gone: the empty chair at the dinner table, the clothes in the closet, a favorite song on the radio.

> **Phase Three**
> *Adaptation*
> Farewell to the Old Life
> The Domino Effect
> Despair
> Reality Check
> Decision Point
> Planning and Action

With realization of the loss begins the struggle to let go of, and, at the same time, hold on to the beloved. One widow describes it as "feeling torn between the past and the future and unable to see the present." One task of this phase is to

| Impact | Chaos | Adaptation | Equilibrium | Transformation |

develop a new way of relating to a lost loved one. Nuland (1997) offers the perspective that "a life may be over from the point of view of time but it is never over from the point of view of emotion." In other words, the relationship with the deceased is never over; it merely takes on a different form.

Many Phoenix Grievers found that conducting a "life review" is an important step in accepting the loss and building a new relationship with the one who has died. The life review should include all aspects of the relationship, both the positive and the negative. This retrospection helps grievers move forward as they revisit their memories and learn to selectively recall and treasure those that bring comfort and strength. They join memories of what they had with the sorrow for what they have lost.

The recollection of positive memories is especially important in helping tragic death images to fade, particularly if a violent death has occurred. Psychologist and author Connierae Andreas (Andreas and Andreas 1989) says, "People often recall the bad times rather than the good times they had with someone they loved. That can make the yearning less, but it also keeps them distant from the positive feelings they had with the lost person. This prevents them from being able to resolve the loss" (p. 110).

It is not unusual in bereavements caused by violent death to find a cluster of symptoms resembling post-traumatic stress, if not the actual clinical state. (Where symptoms of post-traumatic stress are manifested, professional intervention is strongly recommended.) One of the most intrusive is the "flashback," where disturbing mental pictures spontaneously appear, accompanied by feelings of fear, anxiety, and panic. One Phoenix Griever, Norman, who witnessed his child's death, was obsessed by that image. As he became aware that the flashbacks were becoming too intrusive, he sought a means of regaining control.

Impact	Chaos	Adaptation	Equilibrium	Transformation

Norman couldn't bear the constant replays of seeing his son being killed by a hit-and-run driver in front of his eyes. He recalls: "I was truly haunted and thought I was going crazy. I couldn't see anything else when I closed my eyes and sometimes even when they were open.

"Eight months later I went into therapy. A short bout of medication and some integration techniques helped and I began to function better. One of the techniques was not to fight the image. I watched it as if it were on a theater screen and allowed it to pass, followed by a pleasant memory of my son. It gave me some control and helped a lot."

It was only when Norman was able to look beyond the intrusive death images that he could begin to remember the life of his son. As the disturbing images are integrated with happier memories from the loved one's life, the griever can learn to control the appearance of memories and images.

Those who have lost a loved one to a long, drawn-out illness may also have difficulty recalling the loved one before the dying process began. It is painful to have a one-dimensional memory bank.

Michelle remembers: "In the beginning the only memories I could retrieve were of Marie's illness. I kept seeing her with IV's, oxygen, and other tubes, growing paler and weaker by the day. It took a long time to remember the fun and laughter times, and believe me, there were many. These memories strengthen the total picture of my life with my little girl."

Michelle found a way to bring back the happy times with Marie. She created a memory box filled with lovely mementos of her child. She retrieves it whenever she needs to neutralize and balance the negative memories of Marie's illness with recollections of the joy Marie brought to her life. Michelle

| Impact | Chaos | Adaptation | Equilibrium | Transformation |

takes time to "visit" the memory box whenever she needs to feel close to her child. Reviewing the full relationship with the deceased, the good times as well as the bad, is a very important step in integrating the loss and moving forward.

THE DOMINO EFFECT

As the death of the loved one comes to be accepted as fact, the griever often becomes more and more aware of the "domino effect," the secondary losses caused by the death. The death sets off a chain reaction—the toppling of roles and beliefs once associated with the deceased. For instance, with the death of a husband, a widow is no longer defined as part of a couple by society. She loses her identity as a wife, and she loses a companion, a lover, and a primary source of emotional, physical, and socioeconomic support. In other words, the loss of a loved one involves not only a physical absence but also the loss of roles vis-à-vis the deceased.

Barbara, whose husband Mike died suddenly, recalls the domino effect of his death. "It didn't occur to me that I would lose my home because I could no longer afford it. That loss really devastated me and I felt guilty because I grieved for my home. Sometimes I missed my house as much as I missed Mike; my home represented my security and sanctuary and so did he. I forced myself to find something more affordable and eventually felt rather proud of myself for creating a new environment."

During Adaptation, the present and future implications of the loss become more evident. The effects are staggering. These are the reverberatory losses of all that the loved ones meant—the roles they played, the tasks they performed, the responsibilities they assumed, the personality qualities they

| Impact | Chaos | Adaptation | Equilibrium | Transformation |

held, and the ways they contributed to the griever's self-image. As Rando (1993) explains: "Because the death of a loved one brings many losses, what one perceives as a given individual's grief is actually the sum total of all the grief and mourning for each of the losses experienced in connection with the death" (p. 22).

Each loss must be examined and grieved separately until the totality of losses is acknowledged. This takes some time. When grievers face this monumental task, they may quickly become overwhelmed and feel pessimistic about their future.

DESPAIR

During the Impact and Chaos phases, grievers are stunned, then flooded with emotion, and soon overpowered by the magnitude of life changes occurring. In essence, the breakdown of denial, the aftermath of intense emotions, and the dawning awareness of the repercussions of the loss are precursors to feelings of hopelessness.

Too tired to fight their emotions, no longer able to deny the reality of the death, the grievers pass through a cave of despair. This passage is characterized by the temporary suspension of hope—temporary because, in the experience of the Phoenix Grievers, despair is the transition point between before and after, the doorway to life and living.

> Despair is the transition point between before and after, the doorway to life and living.

Maggie felt hopeless, that life had been taken away from her when Ted died. "For me, the feeling of despair was the bridge between hopelessness and hope. I kind of dropped downward into a place where I was aware of all I had lost and simultaneously aware of all that I still had. I began to look at what faced

| Impact | Chaos | Adaptation | Equilibrium | Transformation |

me. Much later I realized that my mind was very busy during that time, even though I was not aware of it."

Until now, the grievers have been looking backward, mourning all that was lost. At this point, what lies ahead begins to dawn on them and the work may feel monumental. A widow asks, "How am I supposed to do everything I do and take on his jobs as well? I can't do it, it's too much. I wish I could go to sleep, wake up, and it would be all gone." A widower with three young children says, "There are more problems than I had imagined. I am doubting my own abilities to handle everything."

Despite appearances to the contrary, grievers are subconsciously preparing themselves to cope and adapt. In bidding farewell to the familiar life with the loved one, now deceased, they must look toward the unfamiliar future and examine what must be created.

Hannah, widowed mother of eight, refused to allow herself to remain in a state of despair. She recognized it very early and said to herself, "I refuse to let the demons of despair take up residence. They are uninvited guests." Shortly thereafter she began to make plans for life without her spouse.

Hannah's awareness of what was happening allowed her to make a choice to either accept or reject the negative emotional environment. She chose not to stay in the cave of despair. She pushed onward.

REALITY CHECK

The reality check can be likened to sorting through the rubble after a natural disaster. It is an assessment of what's left,

| Impact | Chaos | Adaptation | Equilibrium | Transformation |

what must be discarded, and what needs to be done next. The griever must evaluate changes in roles, lifestyle, environment, and relationships with others and with one's self. The hallmark of Adaptation is the confrontation of life without the loved one, and the process is full of questions and doubts.

While consciously despairing, the mourner begins, subconsciously, to generate a realistic model of life without the loved one as well as to envision new ways of being in that life. Such challenges force an individual to grow, and growth in turn demands a reevaluation of one's adaptive strengths and weaknesses. The assessment process serves as an incubator for the redefined self in the redefined world.

New beliefs are forming during this part of Adaptation, but they have not yet been tested. Though not self-confident and not without apprehension about attempting new behaviors at this time, grievers begin to realize that they may have the ability to try out new things. They develop the courage to overcome the barriers of fear and they earn rewards for each accomplishment. Trial and error, trial and success are the building blocks of self-esteem and self-confidence. As Maslow (1968) observed: "We learn also about our own strengths and limits and extend them by overcoming difficulties, by straining ourselves to the utmost, by meeting challenges and hardships, even by failing. Furthermore, this is the best path to healthy self-esteem, which is based not only upon approval from others, but also upon actual achievements and successes and upon the realistic self-confidence which ensues" (p. 200).

Grief often leads us to confront long-held beliefs in an attempt to isolate those that make no sense in light of current events. The rules of life have changed. What appeared to be true no longer is. Dr. Peter Moran (personal communication 1998), authority on cognitive-behavioral therapy, offers an example of the power of beliefs to influence or inhibit growth

| Impact | Chaos | Adaptation | Equilibrium | Transformation |

after the death of a loved one: "Suppose a man loses a life-long mate and he believes that his wife is his whole life and he cannot live without her. Then, at this stage, he is as convinced that he cannot live without his wife any more than he can live without oxygen. This belief, this thought, will destroy any chance he has of living well afterward. The belief must be confronted."

Phoenix Grievers became aware of their beliefs early in their bereavement. They refused to be constrained by negative beliefs and coached themselves continually; the result was a more positive outcome and greater sense of control. According to Moran (1998), "Beliefs have a direct impact on feelings as well as behavior."

For instance, a widowed mother of three realizes that she has to be the income generator and also a strong parental figure to compensate for the loss of her husband. She realizes she will be without a partner, lover, and companion, for now. She considers her options, rejects some and accepts some. She finds a job that allows her to be home early for her children, hires outside help for the handyman chores her husband did, and begins a different lifestyle. First mentally, then physically, she begins to adapt to the situation.

The Adaptation phase is a time for taking mental inventory of what lies ahead and how to meet the challenges healthily. The gaps left by the death of the loved one need to be examined: some can be filled, some cannot. Although mourners may be overwhelmed by myriad tasks, Phoenix Grievers faced the challenges by focusing only on immediate projects. They tried not to act on impulse or out of fear. They delayed long-range plans and allowed things to evolve at a leisurely pace. They sought out expert and non-expert help and support, adapting to the present before plunging into plans for the future.

| Impact | Chaos | Adaptation | Equilibrium | Transformation |

DECISION POINT

From the depths of despair comes a faint whisper of hope. At some level the griever becomes aware that survival without the loved one is more than a dim possibility. Within this quiet, generative phase a decision to try living without the loved one is evolving. The turning point may be so subtle as to take place outside of consciousness.

> At some level, the griever becomes aware that survival without the loved one is more than a dim possibility.

Mark, whose daughter Marie died of cancer, remembers: "It was during the phase of Adaptation that I began to resolve this conflict of living or merely surviving. It was more of a slow evolutionary process where I looked at my life and realized there were two ways to go, one positive, the other negative. I didn't like the negative way, the bitter and pessimistic way, so I chose the other."

Like Mark, many grievers do not recall a dramatic decision point. On the other hand there are others who are acutely aware of the moment that they decided to try living again. That moment of decision to take a risk and re-enter can be among the most profound moments in one's life.

When Bob died, Noella was unemployed and had two small children at home. She recalls the moment when she decided to "make the choice between living as a victim or a survivor. I can still see where I was standing, what I was wearing, who was with me, and what was going on. I hated the feeling of powerlessness, so I decided to make decisions that would give me control over my life and the future of my family. I chose to accept the challenges that life presented, like it or not."

| Impact | Chaos | Adaptation | Equilibrium | Transformation |

Noella's decision to take charge of her life and the responsibility for charting its course came from within her. Others may be shaken out of their despair by some external precipitant, which can be as unexpected as a word, a song, or a chance encounter, or as focused as finding a role model.

Barbara, the widow, recalls her moment of decision. It was during an old World War II movie on a cable channel. "It suddenly occurred to me that here were all these women whose men were off to war and some would never return. Did they mope around feeling sorry for themselves, acting like victims? Hell, no! They searched for purpose and meaning and helped each other through. They carried on their own and the duties of their men. They participated in life even though they knew they could lose their loved ones, and many continued on even when they knew their loved ones had died.

"Where is my spirit, I thought? What happened to me to make me think I couldn't survive without him? He would be so ashamed of me. That was my moment of truth."

Many Phoenix Grievers have been profoundly influenced by considering how their deceased loved ones would regard their attitudes and behaviors. They were able to observe their own progress from that point of view and derive inspiration to forge something constructive from the pain of loss.

Ann, who was 14 when her mother died, recalls: "I was, and am, determined to make her proud of me, wherever she is. This gives me direction. I do the best I can and do not give up. She taught me about morals and strength, how to be strong when I needed to be and when to ask for help. She had a no-nonsense attitude that I imitate. She would want me to stop feeling sorry for myself, after a while of course, and then get going. And that's what I did."

| Impact | Chaos | Adaptation | Equilibrium | Transformation |

Many grievers feel a sense of responsibility to uphold the finer values of their loved ones. Legacies of wisdom, courage, truth, dignity, work ethic, and other values are legacies for the living and are often the stimuli for re-entering the stream of life.

Michelle felt that "It was time to move forward and do something with my life. I owed it to my daughter, my son, and my husband. I owed it to those who had supported and inspired me. Most of all, I recognized that I owed it to myself. I refused to be diminished when Marie had taught me so much about my own strength. She taught me more about courage and love than others learn in a lifetime. It was a stunning revelation and it liberated me. I'm not saying it was easy after that, I'm saying that my commitment to life surfaced and my anxieties around it lessened."

Another powerful force that pulls people out of despair is their love and commitment to others. The fact that they are needed by others, be they family, friends, or strangers, appears to be an important motivational factor.

Joyce, who lost both her daughter and husband, responds to my question about moving out of despair: "How did I do it? I knew only one thing—that I needed to survive because others needed me."

> "How did I do it? I knew only one thing—that I needed to survive because others needed me."

Hope, whose son died by suicide, realized that "My family needed me. There were many things outside of my control, but I could take charge over myself and begin living again. No one could do this for me."

Awareness of the needs of others provides a powerful stimulus toward reconnecting. Responding relieves the lone-

| Impact | Chaos | Adaptation | Equilibrium | Transformation |

liness that is central to the grief experience and helping other people is an attachment tool. Loneliness is a core experience in grief and its remedy is a fundamental task of grieving.

Many grievers have families, friends, and co-workers to assuage feelings of loneliness. Those who are alienated from the community, who have no circle of relationships, must be more resourceful. Volunteering, taking up a new hobby, getting a pet, or joining a group are some of the ways to avoid the pain of loneliness.

During the decision part of Adaptation, grievers come to realize that they alone are accountable for their choices and actions. They are formulating new beliefs based on their experiences with death and grief. They are motivated and inspired by role models, their loved ones' opinions, their own self-images, and the dependencies of others. Many reach a place where their capacity to endure suffering is saturated. They cannot and choose not to withstand any more. Their pain pushes them forward.

Martina, who lost two children, says, "I was sick of it. Sick of the crying, the sadness, the pain, the apathy, the isolation. I told myself—enough! Start the business of living again. I was afraid and excited at the same time. I knew I had to do it or I would never come out of that place called hell."

The cluster of emotions attached to the grief process can be very seductive. Many mourners become accustomed to the pain and fail to move onward. However, fighters like the Phoenix Grievers won't settle for a constricted life. They take action. Their burgeoning awareness of the possibility of a life without their loved ones creates a paradigm shift that takes them forward across the bridge of despair. They move past the midpoint of Adaptation.

Impact	Chaos	Adaptation	Equilibrium	Transformation

PLANNING AND ACTION

Buoyed by the decision to move beyond despair and take action, grievers now begin to create definitive plans. The plans incorporate the results of the reality check taking place throughout the Adaptation phase. They begin to prioritize issues and tasks. They generate timetables for short-term goals. Action may be taken in advance of full readiness, so plans should be reviewed periodically for appropriateness, timeliness, and efficacy.

Michelle planned on going back to school very soon after the death of little Marie. "It was too soon. My grief, fear, and fatigue did not allow me to get past the idea of college. It only generated severe anxiety. I postponed that goal and decided to first stabilize myself and my home situation."

Kristen, whose twins died shortly after birth, went back to work rather quickly. She says, "It is still a regret of mine that I did this. I should have taken more time off to grieve and recover. It didn't seem like I had an option at the time. It was not the wisest thing to do and it did prolong and intensify my grieving. I advise others to take the time to grieve, if possible; even a few days of focusing on your loss will help."

> "I advise others to take the time to grieve, if possible; even a few days of focusing on your loss will help."

It is not unusual for grievers to resume familiar activities, expecting to feel centered and safe by doing so. But the feeling of similarity is an illusion. Life *has* changed. Returning to work, for instance, can be stabilizing but also draining. Often, the breadwinner of the family cannot afford to take the time to grieve that some Phoenix Grievers recommend. On the other hand, the workplace can be a stabilizing, famil-

| Impact | Chaos | Adaptation | Equilibrium | Transformation |

iar atmosphere and may be therapeutic. It could provide the structure needed to adapt to the loss and perhaps a respite from the chaotic emotions. Each person's needs are unique and must be evaluated as such.

How grievers evaluate their needs is crucial to the success of their plan. It takes practice, as with any other new learning. Most mourners will develop a feedback mechanism to tell them whether their choices are helpful or harmful to their adaptation and growth. All the work that has been accomplished prior to this time provides the griever with rudimentary coping and adaptation behaviors.

Initially, a mourner may feel out-of-synch with the rhythm of life. One young bereaved mother recalled: "I felt like others had gone on ahead and I couldn't catch up, let alone know where they were going." A similar sense of alienation and uncertainty occurs during many of life's transitions, such as adolescence, going to college, marriage, and parenthood. During grief these feelings are compounded by fear and emotional anguish and by the rapidity with which they occur. Some grievers can see beyond the anguish to the challenge and the promise of moving forward in new ways.

At the time of her son's suicide, Hope's nursing career had reached an impasse. She says, "It never occurred to me that I had the ability to go further. But after he died, I began to search for ways to strengthen and expand my life. I returned to college and, to my amazement, excelled! I have an updated profession where I can help others at a new level of competency.

"I had no idea that I could be wife, mother, student, professional woman, and supporter to other grievers. My self-confidence and self-esteem kept increasing with each mini-success.

> "My self-confidence and self-esteem kept increasing with each mini-success."

| Impact | Chaos | Adaptation | Equilibrium | Transformation |

"I need to tell you that along the way I exhausted myself several times with unrealistic plans. I had to pull back many times and redo my choices. My adaptation did not proceed in a smooth, linear fashion. I learned about what was right for me and I am still learning."

Hope's observations about taking action and then evaluating the suitability of that choice are important steps in the Planning and Action phase. The Phoenix Grievers are not unique in that they try, but in that they tried *many times* until they achieved a sense of balance, until they felt a healthy sense of self. For these unique individuals, failure at one thing has not meant defeat. It has merely given them new information about themselves and the wisdom of their actions. They began to trust their judgment about what was or wasn't good for them.

David felt emptiness on two fronts: the loss of his daughter and his retirement from the State Department. He says, "I didn't know how to fill my time. Initially, I participated in some self-help groups. That was okay, but not too meaningful. So, I sort of stumbled into the prisoner program led by my minister.

"It was then that I began to get a sense of purpose. It felt right, although not at first. It took a year or more to realize that I had achieved some balance in my life."

Most grievers report feeling awkward in trying out new roles. The feelings of rightness and balance arise as a result of action, not of planning. The same principle applies to one's self-esteem and self-assurance. However, the Phoenix Grievers did not embark on a newly defined life with confidence in their abilities to cope successfully. Their skills grew in response to each challenge they faced. Each step forward, each risk taken, each task accomplished, empowered them.

| Impact | Chaos | Adaptation | Equilibrium | Transformation |

Some grievers are catapulted into action through circumstances beyond their control. Multiple sequential deaths foreshorten the time to fully grieve and arrive at the point of action. Before they can resolve one death they are hit with another. In these situations, Chaos and Adaptation intermingle because action must be taken immediately.

Elizabeth needed to act quickly, taking charge of her young grandson after the deaths of her daughter, son-in-law and granddaughter. "It was not that I didn't grieve—bitterly—but I had to confine it to small spurts of pain when I wasn't occupied with the care of this young survivor of the crash. Over the past few years, I continue to grieve and maybe it's taking longer because I can't get enough of it accomplished. But, that's the way it is. My life is beginning to balance now, and for that I am grateful."

Elizabeth was also immersed in legal proceedings involving the fatal accident. Legal aspects of any death may seriously disrupt the normal progression of the grief process. This complication suggests the need for a skilled therapist.

Another factor leading to postponing grief is responsibility to others. The so-called strong ones in a family system will often jump right in to meet and stabilize the crisis situation. They may delay processing their own grief until such time when it erupts, unless they are aware of the importance of returning to confront it. Often, it may catch them off-guard.

Patty, whose husband died in a plane crash, was the strong one and now the sole parent. "I knew I had to cope. The kids needed me to take charge. I had to pull away and push down my grief. There were too many other demands on my time and emotions.

"Well, the grief finally blew, just like a volcano. It happened when our dog died. I think the well of grief just overflowed and

| Impact | Chaos | Adaptation | Equilibrium | Transformation |

I cried for many days. I was so scared that I went into therapy. Dealing with my painful emotions was exhausting but it was also the beginning of healing."

Caregivers, nurturers, and "strong ones" will identify with Patty's superwoman expectations and with her subsequent perceptions. Today's society demands all we have to give under the most normal circumstances. The additional burden of a loved one's death is devastating. Recognizing and acknowledging the need for help entails the griever's redefining beliefs about his or her capabilities.

> Today's society demands all we have to give under the most normal circumstances. The additional burden of a loved one's death is devastating.

There are others for whom jumping into action and pushing grief aside is not altogether a bad move. For them it is a necessary postponement. It is important for them to realize that grief is waiting backstage while the action is taking place onstage. Awareness of motive, choice, and behavior is fundamental to dealing effectively with postponed grief.

Whether grievers' action plans are realistic or idealistic, helpful or harmful, short-term or long-term, they are a beginning to living without the loved one. They can and should be modified to reflect ongoing life changes. Grievers enter the phase of Adaptation in a state of despair and leave with a budding sense of confidence. Adaptation is a time of experimentation.

GRIEF WORK

Adaptation provides the framework with which the griever begins living without the loved one. It is the beginning

| Impact | Chaos | Adaptation | Equilibrium | Transformation |

of "after" while moving away from "before." During this phase, order and structure are forming from the elements of chaos. Both internal and external perceptual shifts must occur in order to cope with the loss and adapt to the new reality.

Now is the time when mourners begin to perceive themselves in a different way. They are challenged to re-examine and redefine some of their former thoughts, beliefs, and behaviors. In this way, the person becomes both the architect and the contractor for this poignant project. Bear in mind that the work is taking place when grievers have the least energy and motivation because they are still experiencing the painful emotions and turbulence of the phase of Chaos. Yet, they must adapt if life is to assume a meaningful pattern.

Grievers need to be their own coaches and cheerleaders to elicit and sustain a modicum of enthusiasm and motivation for the new challenges. They will have to make realistic short-term plans and tolerate the frustration of attempting something new. However, the challenge of Adaptation is not without its rewards. Grievers acquire self-confidence and self-esteem through this and the next phases.

FOR THE GRIEVER

Phoenix Grievers suggest the following:

- Continue with your previous wellness routine.
- Examine the beliefs you hold about your own capabilities. Begin to redefine negative ones. Try to get help with this project.
- Seek positive role models for growth. Others have done this and so can you.
- Make realistic plans. Do not leap too far into the future.

| Impact | Chaos | Adaptation | Equilibrium | Transformation |

- Do not get discouraged. Frustration is part of trying out the unfamiliar.
- Remember, failure is not defeat. Your initial choice may not have been the right one for you or you may need more time or practice. Let go of whatever isn't working. Go back to the drawing board.
- Activate prayer and meditation. It helps to look at your faith and spirituality even through your anger and pain.
- Look for ways to integrate your loved one into your internal and external life. Ask yourself "what would (he or she) want me to do?" or "How would (she or he) have handled this?"
- Reassure and coach yourself, daily, that you can and you will get through this. Never give up hope.

FOR THE THERAPIST

Most of the shock, denial, and disbelief sequelae have dissipated by this time because the aftermath of the death is all too real. The emotional and physical signs of distress as well as the perceptual turbulence of the phase of Chaos are still apparent. For some they may be waning, while others may still be experiencing the acute symptoms of grief as the tasks of Adaptation are imposed on them. As we examine the Phoenix Model, we see that Adaptation, Chaos, and Equilibrium overlap at their boundaries.

In examining the Maslow model during Adaptation, we notice that the safety needs (shelter, food, water, sleep) have been met. The security needs (freedom from fear and anxiety, predictability, familiarity) may still be surfacing, the belonging needs (attachment, order, loving) are emerging, and the esteem needs (risking, trying, succeeding, confidence) are beginning to be filled.

| Impact | Chaos | Adaptation | Equilibrium | Transformation |

Therapists should continue to monitor the griever for signs and symptoms of real emotional and physical distress. Appropriate treatment and/or referral should be initiated at this point in order to reduce the risks of complicated mourning.

The time has come to soft-pedal the crisis intervention approach and accelerate other modalities, such as cognitive-behavioral and brief, solution-oriented psychotherapy. Sequence counts, because a griever will not be able to respond to cognitive-behavioral, rational-emotive, or reality therapy modalities while in the acute state of emotional cathexis (Chaos) or shock (Impact), nor will he need crisis intervention when he is successfully meeting the challenges of new roles. All of the suggested interventions need to be filtered through a warm, genuine, authentic persona, regardless of which is chosen, in keeping with the therapist's personality and training.

Grievers are attempting to adjust to and create a life without the loved one. Frustration, sorrow, anger, loneliness, and anxiety are predominant emotions. The therapist should carefully assess and gently explain the bottoming-out component of despair, and assist them with realistic plans based on their unique life circumstances while honoring their individuality. The turbulence of the phase of Chaos is beginning to decrease in frequency and intensity at this time. Probable exceptions would be during significant grief sojourns such as anniversary dates and holidays when the mourner is in a vulnerable state, albeit briefly. Therapists should:

- **Listen:** Attend to the griever's unique representation of the meaning of the loss and the challenges of his/her adaptation.
- **Assess:** Evaluate the griever's needs and challenges according to the Phoenix Model of grief.

Impact	Chaos	Adaptation	Equilibrium	Transformation

Table 7–1. The Phoenix Model of Grief: Adaptation Phase

Needs	Tasks	Intervention
For:	*To:*	*Use:*
All base level needs	Maintain physiological and emotional stability	A more directive and solution-oriented approach in a humanistic manner
	Continue to acknowledge and express the emotions of grief	Supportive and facilitative methods
Belonging	Connect with others; beware of isolation	Referral network, if necessary
		Guidance toward community resources for support and advice
Self-esteem	Develop a sense of self and place in the world through risk taking and developing new roles	Cognitive-behavioral techniques for growth-inhibiting beliefs
		Supportive, solution-oriented models

- **Normalize:** Reassure the griever of the normality of the manifestations of this aspect of grief because validation brings reassurance and encouragement.
- **Plan:** Create, with the griever, a realistic outline for adapting to the world without the loved one. Continue to encourage emotional expression.
- **Intervene:** Prioritize therapeutic issues and treatment. Stabilize, link to a support team, support and encourage realistic plans. Use cognitive-behavioral techniques

| Impact | Chaos | Adaptation | Equilibrium | Transformation |

for "barrier-beliefs," which prevent the griever from moving forward in life.

- **Support:** Endorse the griever's suggestions for healthy reactive and proactive adaptation to life without the loved one.
- **Educate:** Explain the level of progress in a developmental context. Use the Phoenix Model handout.
- **Monitor:** Be alert for serious depression or other complications. Be proactive and assertive if untoward symptoms are developing. Design strategies for intervention in this most pivotal phase of grief.

SUMMARY

- The phase of adaptation focuses on living without the loved one.
- The griever moves from the past with the beloved, through the present, and into the future without the beloved.
- This is one of the most crucial of all phases. It brings the griever into risk-taking, belief-confrontation, early development of self-esteem, and self-confidence.
- This is an especially lonely time when support systems greatly mitigate fear, panic, and anxiety. Mentors and role models of positive grief outcome are invaluable supports.

But some of the grievers did not emerge from the darkness of the cave where light cannot enter.

Some grew frightened and went back without completing their journeys. Others remained in the cave, paralyzed by their own fear.

| Impact | Chaos | Adaptation | Equilibrium | Transformation |

Those who followed their guides found hope, and exited from the cave into a place they hadn't imagined. . . .

| Impact | Chaos | Adaptation | Equilibrium | Transformation |

8

Rising from the Ashes: Phase Four—Equilibrium

And it came to pass that the journey was approaching its completion and the grievers marveled at how the passage had changed them. . . .

The griever's transition into Equilibrium is almost seamless. Yet there is an imperceptible evolution taking place. This is an active period of adding additional pieces to the self, integrating the new ones, and testing out the composite. The central core of the griever's personality remains intact and the new layers form around it, much like onion skins.

The grievers are developing fresh images of themselves that will greatly influence their future growth. As they successfully meet new challenges, their feelings of mastery and empowerment continue to develop. They form new beliefs about their own strengths, weaknesses, talents, and interests. Through the frustration of trial and error, they choose what works for them and what reflects their developing self-esteem. The world becomes a mirror that reflects their changes.

Life resumes its consistent rhythm as the person enters the fourth phase of grief, Equilibrium. During the earlier

| Impact | Chaos | Adaptation | Equilibrium | Transformation |

parts of this phase, the griever's balance is constantly being challenged. Later, it stabilizes. The person is beginning to be more comfortable with herself and her new way of being in this world. Let us explore the elements and hypothetical sequence of the grief work of this phase.

REHEARSING

As Equilibrium unfolds, grievers find that just getting through the day and being able to function is enough. It takes a lot of their energy to try out new thoughts and behaviors. Gradually, this laborious effort tempers. Changes become easier as the Phoenix Grievers build their self-confidence and self-awareness.

Phase Four:
Equilibrium
Rehearsing
Integration
Taking Risks
Beliefs
Forgiveness
Spirituality
Grief Revisited
The End of Mourning?

Michelle, whose daughter Marie died, recalls that "Initially, I restored order to my home life. I established a firm connection to my son and my husband. Then I began to add small outside interests, ever aware of when I was feeling stressed. I feel more centered now because I know myself better and I am aware of when I am out of balance."

Michelle paid attention to what her mind and body were telling her about choices and changes. Feedback from within guided her toward her own personal balance in life. Before the deaths of their loved ones, Phoenix Grievers were motivated and directed by their old scripts and the expectations of others. Most of them didn't examine or question their assigned roles. At this time they find themselves developing new roles with more confidence. Now, the incentive comes from

Impact	Chaos	Adaptation	Equilibrium	Transformation

within as they respond to their inner voices. They also seem to gravitate toward healthier, more positive choices.

The precarious steps toward balance are constantly being challenged. Walking the new path begins on wobbly legs. Rehearsing the new script transports the griever to a new level of frustration tolerance. The earlier part of this phase is not without its triumphs or its setbacks.

Lorna, whose husband Mike died suddenly, affirms this statement and adds: "Sometimes I feel that I take three steps forward and one step backward. I have, nevertheless, gained two steps. I feel that every day is a growing process for me whether it is positive or negative. Negative actions can also contribute to growth. I believe in myself now and I continue to grow. I know I can make it!"

Lorna expresses the Phoenix Grievers' sentiment that negative feedback is as growth inducing as is positive, since all feedback provides information upon which to make decisions or to correct decisions already made. Having the courage to find and pursue the individually right patterns is the key to growth for each person. Persistence and practice lead the griever to familiarity with the new roles and the griever's life stabilizes as balance is attained.

Inherent in this phase is an underlying commitment to developing a new way of being in the world. Even though Phoenix Grievers may not be consciously aware of it, they are drafting a covenant to live without the loved one. This resolution brings forth direction, purpose, and responsibility.

Amy, whose twin brother Jeffrey was killed when they were 19 years old says, "All my life I had my insurance policy against loneliness, I had Jeffrey. When he died, I had no direction, I was lost. Then the time came when I chose to continue my life with-

| Impact | Chaos | Adaptation | Equilibrium | Transformation |

out him. I stayed in college, volunteered to tutor, made new friends, and committed myself to the future and to living my own life. I knew no one could do this for me. I had to take responsibility now that he was gone. It is good now, my life is full and I know where I'm going and how to get there."

Planning a life without the loved one requires many components: commitment, responsibility, direction, forethought, determination, and courage. The Phoenix Grievers add the necessary resources as they continue through the fourth phase, Equilibrium.

INTEGRATION

Important to this phase is the concept that the old familiar pieces of the self are retained and new pieces interwoven, so that no part of the personality is ever lost. Every experience that has shaped a person's essence becomes a resource. We constantly weave new threads into the tapestry of our selves and synthesize them in such a way that the developing personality is simultaneously familiar and strange.

Noella says of her own integration: "Everything I have developed during those difficult years has helped me shape my future. It's with me every day. It's now part of who I am. I believe that as we grow and change throughout our lives, we learn to keep what works well for us and change those things that do not."

There is a time for each resource to be used and the mature, self-aware individual applies the right one at the right time. During the process of grief we are sorting out which resources do not work for us, which ones do, and when to use

| Impact | Chaos | Adaptation | Equilibrium | Transformation |

them. What may have worked in the past, such as having a temper tantrum at age two, most likely will not get us what we need in the present.

Integration is very much about balance. As the negatives are examined, they are neutralized by positive and life-affirming attributes. These attitudes may arise from grievers' efforts to create meaning, symbolically. They take into themselves certain qualities, characteristics, and interests of their lost loved one through a process called introjection. In this way, they give homage to the positive aspects of their loved ones' personalities. Recall Ann, whose mother died, as she consciously chose to imitate her mother's no-nonsense approach to life and a doing-the-best-you-can attitude. Remember Carole, indulged daughter, who became a physician. She modeled her caregiving and unselfishness after her deceased father. And Scott, who brought forth the qualities unmanifest in his father: honor, devotion, and pride. In this manner, the loved one's memory remains in the world, influencing others in a positive manner.

Phoenix Grievers report having fewer feelings of intolerance, prejudice, and generalized anxieties. An individual who was critical, sarcastic, and fearful of life before the trauma of the death of the loved one will confront and neutralize negative qualities with tolerance, affirmation, and trust.

This is not to say that Phoenix Grievers are saint-like. They are very human. They are authentic and honest about themselves and others. Through the grieving process they have developed depth of character, coping skills, insight, and a broader perspective about themselves and their relationship with this world. Endowed with more choices for responding to life's demands and challenges, they are more adaptable. And, endowed with strengths forged from tragic circumstances, they are more mature.

Impact	Chaos	Adaptation	Equilibrium	Transformation

Before his father committed suicide, Scott lacked direction in life and the maturity to make decisions. "Before my father's death I was trying to find my way in life. I didn't have a clue. His death forced me to grow in a way that matured me quickly.

"I headed in a career direction that I never expected. The strengths and talents I had were blended, in some way, with the new qualities I developed through grieving his death. I became different, yet I was also the same. I am amazed at this. I became a state trooper and my need to help others has an outlet that is good."

It is not unusual to hear a Phoenix Griever express astonishment at the path taken in life because of the death of a loved one. Tragedies precipitate a perceptual shift and the griever does not necessarily see the world or life in the same way as before. Many grievers who had been heading in one direction in life find themselves redirected after the death of a loved one. The results cannot always be predicted.

> Many grievers who had been heading in one direction in life find themselves redirected after the death of a loved one.

Carole was 20 years old when her controlling, indulgent father died. She was "very spoiled and totally self-centered. My father parented me the only way he knew how. I guess he thought he was protecting me.

"My abilities for empathy and compassion must have been dormant because I finished my next two years of college as premed and went to medical school. Something happened to point me in that direction; that something was the death of my father."

How to explain what happened to Carole? What moved such a spoiled person to become a doctor? Whether she had a strong internal drive to balance her selfish traits with unself-

| Impact | Chaos | Adaptation | Equilibrium | Transformation |

ish dedication, or whether the death of her father altered her perception of the purpose of her own life, Carole was able to access her dormant abilities: compassion, commitment, and self-discipline. Phoenix Grievers consistently report such a push toward balance and harmony. Each barrier hurdled as they move through the levels of grief involves taking a risk.

TAKING RISKS

Maslow (1968) says, "We learn also about our strengths and limits and extend them by overcoming difficulties, by straining ourselves to the utmost, by meeting challenges and hardships, even by failing. Furthermore, this is the best path to healthy self-esteem, which is based not only upon approval from others, but also upon actual achievements and successes and upon the realistic self-confidence which ensues" (p. 200).

The Phoenix Grievers continue developing self-confidence and self-esteem by facing challenges, overriding fears, and tolerating the frustrations of adopting new choices and behaviors.

Phoenix Grievers overcame fears as they approached risky choices. Fear of the unfamiliar is one barrier to be hurdled. Many grievers face the formidable task of attaining independence after having been taken care of by another, the deceased.

Noella was the prototypical housewife and mother when Bob died. "My life was no different than every other woman I knew—my mother, my sisters, my friends. The women stayed home and took care of their families. In turn, they were taken care of. That was the deal.

"Well, the deal fell through. There was no longer a breadwinner, no longer someone to take care of me and no longer was there a daddy for the children. It was up to me. I was terrified. I had to push past the fear. I didn't allow myself a different choice.

| Impact | Chaos | Adaptation | Equilibrium | Transformation |

"I ventured into the strange new world of college and became a professional woman. No woman in my family has ever accomplished this feat. Now I am quite capable of taking care of myself and my family. If I had not pushed through the fear, I cannot imagine what would have happened."

Phoenix Grievers echo the conviction that pushing past fear is a pivotal step toward building the new self. This action adds resources to the emerging personality. As each impediment is overcome, grievers become stronger and more confident in their abilities to meet subsequent challenges.

Michelle's experiences with pregnancies had been burdened with sorrow. Yet, after losing little Marie, she and Mark wanted another child. She says, "I was terrified to face the decision I had been putting off. Yet, I knew the time was now. Because it was difficult for me to conceive, I needed more determination to overcome my fears.

"Finally, I became pregnant. And with it came its own set of questions, anxieties, and challenges. This is the way of life. Anything worth risking, especially love, means facing fear. For me, it is far worse a fate not to risk loving, for that would not be living."

> "This is the way of life. Anything worth risking, especially love, means facing fear."

The challenge to risk loving again is a familiar one to Phoenix Grievers and a particularly threatening one. For many, it is the ultimate danger, which they want to avoid confronting for as long as possible, if not forever. To arrive at the decision to do so, Phoenix Grievers had to face the fear and summon the courage to go beyond it. This involved redefining some of their previously held beliefs.

Impact	Chaos	Adaptation	Equilibrium	Transformation

BELIEFS

The Phoenix Grievers have described some of the beliefs they held until the time of their losses. Most carry themes of reward and punishment ("I'm being punished for my sins") and themes of guarantee ("If I follow all the rules, nothing bad will happen") or irrational laws ("Death doesn't come until you are old"). Obviously these beliefs collapse in the face of life events of which random death is one. Catastrophic events, untimely deaths, multiple tragedies are all part of life's inconstancies.

Moran (personal communication 1998) says, "Your beliefs, your thoughts profoundly influence how you feel and how you behave. They control your motivation and how you live your life. The challenge now facing grievers is to have the courage to open up new ways of redefining their beliefs. The process of grief offers that opportunity."

Phoenix Grievers have struggled with their beliefs and have built new ones. One noteworthy belief that carries a potential for lifetime suffering is that parents can always protect their children. A mother whose daughter was murdered has realistically adjusted her beliefs: "Tragedy strikes anyone no matter how good a parent you were or tried to be. We are all vulnerable." A grieving father, who believed he could prevent his child from being harmed, says, "I believe that children do not belong to their parents; they belong to God. They are merely on loan to us." A young widow, who has not given in to disillusionment, adds, "I believe bad things happen, but so do good things and they are all part of life. Why are we surprised at this duality?"

As Phoenix Grievers examine and revise their previously held beliefs, the new versions are rooted in their personal experiences with loss and grief. They share their new ideology.

| Impact | Chaos | Adaptation | Equilibrium | Transformation |

Deborah, whose daughter died in a motor vehicle accident, recalls: "I believed that I would never be the same again, because that's what I was told. I wondered about going through this pain. What was it all for?

"Nobody told me that I would be different—better, wiser, more loving, more able to show true forgiveness and compassion for others. Nobody told me that I would have the strength to build a life with much more meaning in it. This is what I now believe and it is what I personally know."

> "Nobody told me that I would have the strength to build a life with much more meaning in it."

Julian, whose brother died in a skiing accident, held the stereotypical beliefs about men and grief. "I was taught that men need to be strong, not to cry, and to go back to work right away. I actually delayed my grieving process for almost a year in this way. Then it caught up with me. I firmly believe that letting myself completely feel the pain when it came was the beginning of my healing and it is a natural process. Living by others' beliefs does not always work."

"Grief is an ongoing ingredient of life," says Noella, "just as much as joy and sorrow and triumph and tragedy. How we respond to life's challenges makes our lives richer or poorer."

Emma, whose three sons and one grandson died, resolutely believes that "grief and life go together. They are and always will be part of each other."

Dianna, whose daughter Grace died of leukemia, now believes that "Bereavement is forever. You learn to live with it with dignity.

> "Bereavement . . . is a part of loving and remembering and honoring your loved one for the rest of your life."

| Impact | Chaos | Adaptation | Equilibrium | Transformation |

It is a part of loving and remembering and honoring your loved one for the rest of your life."

The construction of new beliefs relies heavily on an accurate perception of what life is all about. This means the good, the bad and the ugly. Ultimately, the Phoenix Grievers came to believe in themselves as instruments of love, compassion, and courage. "Life is what it is. My responsibility to myself and others is to realize that and to be the strongest and best person I can be to handle it," declares a griever who has lost several loved ones. This natural progression of changing beliefs leads to the germination of a personal spirituality. Many Phoenix Grievers began this process with the work of forgiveness.

FORGIVENESS

One critical element of spirituality is the concept of forgiveness. The fetters of guilt, bitterness, hurt, rage, and retaliation are emotional and spiritual burdens. Forgiving someone to whom we no longer have an earthly connection may seem like a formidable task. Robin Casarjian, author of *Forgiveness: A Bold Choice for a Peaceful Heart* says, "I don't believe we are disconnected because a person dies physically. Regardless of whether a person is alive or dead we still are left with the fallout of unresolved emotions. As a result, we remain bound despite the fact the person has died. By forgiving, we free ourselves to be more peaceful, to be happier, and to be more spiritually connected" (1997 personal communication). Casarjian (1992) further states: "The most obvious reason for forgiving is to relieve ourselves of the debilitating effects of chronic anger and resentment" (p. 15). It is evident that for-

| Impact | Chaos | Adaptation | Equilibrium | Transformation |

giveness is a cleansing process for grievers and disconnects them from the tire-
some burdens they have been carrying.
Casarjian continues: "Forgiving yourself
is probably the greatest challenge you
will ever meet" (p. 135).

> "Forgiving
> yourself is
> probably the
> greatest challenge
> you will ever meet."
> —Casarjian

Cassandra, who was the caregiver for her mother, says, "I
was more often than not impatient with her. I was exhausted,
cranky, and irritable. I was not always sensitive to her needs. I
can never change that. I wish I could. But I am working on understanding how exhaustion influences your behavior and, in that
way, forgive myself. I know my mother would."

Phoenix Grievers felt that it was very difficult to forgive
themselves. They had not realized the power of their own unrealistic standards of accountability: that loving someone
cannot protect him from dying. As mourners advance in the
grieving process, they begin to view themselves as more human, vulnerable, and imperfect, and, ironically, this is liber-
ating for them.

Joyce, whose daughter's suicide was followed by the death
of her husband, reflects on forgiveness: "I spent considerable
time brooding over what I could have done to prevent either of
these events. I finally came to realize that I simply did not have
the power to have intervened. I forgave myself for being human
and for being powerless."

It may take a lot of work to come to terms with a realistic
view of personal accountability. So many of us carry guilt,
remorse, shame, and often self-punishment for deeds that
were not within our control. Self-punishment may lead to

| Impact | Chaos | Adaptation | Equilibrium | Transformation |

beliefs about being undeserving and behaviors that are neglectful or unhealthy.

Forgiveness can also set another free. Someone who has directly or indirectly caused another person's death is judged guilty in the hearts of those who mourn the victim. A judgment of guilty leads to expectations of justice. If justice is not meted out by the system, how does the griever deal with thoughts and feelings of retribution? Is it possible to transcend vengeance and forgive the person responsible for a loved one's death? Few individuals have the spiritual strength to exhibit compassion and forgiveness in these situations. This Phoenix Griever did.

Deborah's daughter Anna died in an automobile accident in which Anna's boyfriend was driving. He was found to be at fault and was about to be sentenced to prison when Deborah presented an impassioned plea before the judge. "I asked the judge to show compassion and sentence this suffering young man to probation dedicated to many hours of community service. I pleaded with him that there not be any more victims from this tragic event. Instead, let others be helped through his service.

"The judge honored my request and the young man is a finer person today. In my heart I knew he was behaving less than responsibly when the accident occurred. Yet, how many of us have acted irresponsibly with no tragic consequences?"

Deborah's act of forgiveness is a rare and beautiful one. It began in her heart and extended outward to embrace someone whose pain she recognized as kin to her own. Rather than deliver more pain and suffering she offered comfort and hope to another griever from the depths of her own wounds. This was not an instantaneous forgiveness. It emerged over time

| Impact | Chaos | Adaptation | Equilibrium | Transformation |

through much deliberation. Deborah allowed the young man to demonstrate what I term *creative atonement.*

CREATIVE ATONEMENT

This term refers to the use of guilt and remorse over a perceived wrong to create something beneficial. It is a deed that transcends forgiveness. It promotes healing in both the forgiver and the forgiven. When Deborah petitioned the judge for clemency in passing sentence, the young man was able to begin atoning for a tragedy that took a life by aiding other lives. This was not effortless. It took courage and determination because he, too, was grieving.

Casarjian's work with prisoners ("lifers") demonstrates creative atonement in action. In a recent interview (personal communication 1997) she explains: "In my work on forgiveness and healing with prisoners, men who have committed homicide have really used their time in prison to try to turn their lives around. They actually bring youth at risk into the prison for counseling, encouragement, and support. The lifers are using their lives very constructively so that these youth won't end up where they are."

It is important to realize that forgiveness does not excuse or condone a wrongful act. It is a conscious choice to let go of the ties that bind us to the perpetrator of the act. It entails a new understanding and a changed perception of the person who has hurt us, while not excusing the behaviors that brought us pain. Forgiveness brings healing and leads the griever closer to a spiritual balance.

> It is important to realize that forgiveness does not excuse or condone a wrongful act.

| Impact | Chaos | Adaptation | Equilibrium | Transformation |

David's daughter was raped and murdered. When he began volunteering at the state prison, he certainly was not looking to forgive. There, in that place where hope is in short supply, he was surrounded by men like the one who had killed his daughter, Ruth.

"After awhile, I began to forgive the man who did this terrible thing. But it wasn't a real forgiveness. It wasn't a real healing. It was just a word without meaning. The real thing took much longer."

It may take years for the feelings to catch up with the intent to forgive. Casarjian says, "It is very important for people to realize that forgiveness is usually not a one-time event. We can genuinely forgive someone and an hour later feel angry at him." Forgiveness is a process within the larger process of grief. It can span the entire experience of grieving and is not necessarily confined to one phase.

According to clinical psychologist Dr. John Pelletier (personal communication 1998), the process of forgiveness includes acknowledging the pain, committing to let go of the pain, and activating the process. He believes that healing can be greatly enhanced by the griever's willingness to express the pain verbally, to expel its toxicity. He advocates the use of journals, audiotapes, self-talk, talking with trusted others, and praying.

Dr. Pelletier emphasizes the importance of depersonalizing the painful event because it says more about the perpetrator than the victim. It is not the fault of the victim; it is the pathology of the perpetrator. This latter point is of considerable help in neutralizing the shame and self-blame that accompany victimization.

Dr. Pelletier admonishes grievers to be patient with themselves, mindful of the fact that forgiveness may take a long

| Impact | Chaos | Adaptation | Equilibrium | Transformation |

time to accomplish. When it happens, it releases the griever from an unhealthy bondage to negative emotions that serve no useful purpose.

Traveling the road to wellness, the Phoenix Grievers realize that forgiveness encompasses lesser offenses as well as more significant ones. One transgression that Phoenix Grievers feel unanimous about is the lack of sensitivity by others toward grievers, as revealed by attitudes, verbalizations, and actions or non-actions (avoidance). Although grievers may understand the discomfort or general ineptitude of non-grievers, they still feel hurt and/or angry. Family members and friends of grievers who intend to make the griever feel better may fail miserably. Many times, saying nothing but giving a hug and being there to listen is enough.

Kristen recalls: "When my twin babies died, I really expected sensitivity and support from my friends. I was disappointed, hurt, and angry when they avoided talking about my losses. I needed to talk but others did not want to listen or ask how I was. It was as if my children had never existed.

"I don't know which was worse, their not talking or saying stupid things like 'You're young, you'll have others. It's not like you've had them for years you know. Get on with your life. God wanted them with Him.' I mean, really, how dumb can people be? How do you respond to statements like that?

"It took me a long time to step into their shoes and realize they didn't know what to say or do. I let go of my anger and forgave them and forgave myself for judging them."

True forgiveness arises from a seed germinating in the soul, takes root in the mind as a thought, and blooms into a word or deed. Every step toward forgiveness forms a building block of spirituality.

Impact	Chaos	Adaptation	Equilibrium	Transformation

SPIRITUALITY

This part of grief work encompasses many hours of soul searching devoted to seeking life's purpose, creating meaning in one's own life, and developing or refining a concept of the Almighty. By now, grievers are beginning to give form to a new spirituality based on the reality of their experiences, weaving together the old and the new. A new and trusting faith, one that offers no earthly guarantees, is evolving. Jackson (1961) defines this faith very nicely: "Faith does not operate on the immature promise of seeking what we want in life as much as it seeks to make something fine of what life brings to us. It knows the importance of creative adjustment to the circumstances we do not make but must accept" (p. 63).

There is no doubt that having a firm belief in a higher power and trust in the purpose of life events will comfort and support a griever. Dr. Allen Ward (personal communication 1997), Director of Hospice, Worcester, MA, affirms this statement: "Religious faith cultivates courage and strength in those who are dying and those who are mourning. Those with a true spiritual connection to a Greater Being seem to be more empowered to withstand life's adversities." As an oncologist, Dr. Ward has observed people's responses to tragedies for many years. He believes that true spirituality sustains the body and the soul.

True spirituality differs from "hand-me-down religious teachings," in one griever's words. When people find comfort in the tenets of their original faith, that is fine; when they do not, however, their spirituality may be severely challenged or destroyed when a loved one dies. So, when people formulate their spirituality based on the reality of their own experiences, it is just as fine. Having a sense of comfort is the most important thing. Spirituality fills the void which David, the

| Impact | Chaos | Adaptation | Equilibrium | Transformation |

bereaved father, calls "a hole in the soul." Michelle, bereaved mother, describes it differently.

Michelle considers herself a product of inflexible religious tenets. "What I knew before about God was second-hand. It was passed on from generation to generation in my family. I accepted it without question.

"When Marie died, I was left with shattered faith. I had only questions and no answers. It's been a long process of discovering who God is for me. In college, I met a priest who helped me reconfigure my concept of God. Now I know that my child is with an all-loving God who also gives me the strength and wisdom to fully live my own given life span."

Tragedies will critically test grievers' spirituality. The unexpected experience of the loss of a loved one shatters preconceived beliefs and challenges grievers to create a custom-designed set of spiritual truths.

Phoenix Grievers struggle with their fractured spirituality. They attempt to reconnect with a higher power, but in many cases feel contentment about God only if their expectations are met. In some way, they impose conditions on their allegiance to their deity. If God behaves according to their beliefs, then they will love and honor Him. Their expectations are high but their disillusionment is higher when a tragedy strikes. The concept of a benevolent God coupled with a senseless tragedy doesn't make sense.

Gary, whose wife and child were killed, asked himself, "What kind of a God allows this senseless tragedy to occur? What kind of a monster would do this? I didn't want anything to do with this God, this traitor, this betrayer of my trust."

Gary had believed that he and his family were safe as long as they did the "right things." He explains, "I thought God was

| Impact | Chaos | Adaptation | Equilibrium | Transformation |

in charge, but I grew to realize that He expected me to take control over my own responses to life.

"This may sound odd but I feel safer believing that I can and will handle and overcome anything that life presents. I'll always have His love and someday I expect to be with Kim and Sarah again. Until that time, I'll live my life to make them proud."

Many Phoenix Grievers believe that God provides the sustenance and comfort to allow them to face trials and tribulations in life. "It's like we are the engines and God provides the fuel," says a young widow. One of the most persuasive thoughts about the emergence of heroic and unselfish qualities through adversity comes from Rabbi Harold Kushner, author of *When Bad Things Happen to Good People* (1981). He says: "I had to ask myself where they got those qualities which they would freely admit they did not have before. My answer is that this is one of the ways in which God helps us when we suffer beyond the limits of our own strength" (p. 142).

Others feel an inner substantiality that reassures them they will be able to handle anything that comes their way ("God would never give me more than I could deal with."). They feel that God monitors suffering so that no individual receives more than his or her allotted share. Yet sometimes, the number of tragedies one person suffers seems inconsistent with that thought.

Emma, a cheerful, helpful, and outgoing woman, does not appear to have had more than her share of loss and grief. She radiates love and captivates people with the warmth of her personality. Yet, Emma has experienced the deaths of three sons, one grandson, and, most recently, her husband. She says, "I don't blame God for these tragedies. I don't know why, but I have a strong faith. There are reasons for things happening that will never be understood.

Impact	Chaos	Adaptation	Equilibrium	Transformation

"There are also the miracles of what we have, but we have to look for them. I look at the living ones in my life and give thanks. Love is what we have. I believe that life is eternal and love is immortal."

Emma's words pierce the heart with their elegant purity. Losses that would extinguish the spark in many of our hearts become a flame of purpose and meaning in a Phoenix Griever like Emma. Her life is balanced, serene, and spiritual. She believes in the timelessness of love and knows she will be reunited with her loved ones again. Meanwhile, as her time on earth continues, she will make the best of it by fulfilling her potential.

Another spiritual channel that brings comfort and connection to the Phoenix Grievers is praying or talking to their loved ones.

Paul, who was 20 when his father died, describes his unrivaled viewpoint. "Well, I watched this program about saints interceding with God. I figured that my father could just as easily intercede for me as any saint. I used to pick up the phone to talk to him every day. Now I just pick up a different kind of celestial phone."

Paul expresses a fine approach to redefining and integrating his father into his present life. Many share his point of view about having a personal intermediary or "guardian angel" in the afterlife. Many Phoenix Grievers are comforted by the belief that there is a loved one who looks after them and is responsive to their communications and requests.

The majority of Phoenix Grievers believe in life after life. They are convinced that when the soul can no longer be sustained within our earthly space suit, it moves on, free and unencumbered, into a different domain.

| Impact | Chaos | Adaptation | Equilibrium | Transformation |

Lorna feels that "I am more aware of the existence of the spirit of loved ones which goes on after death. I feel that there is a residual entity which continues to exist. I feel more spiritual but less religious."

Lorna makes a distinction between religious and spiritual. Many Phoenix Grievers express the same differentiation and emphasize their development of a personal relationship with God. They describe the destruction of the old and the subsequent construction of the new spirituality as infiltrating the entire grief process. As their spiritual evolution continues, they relate differently to their higher power, much as a child relates differently to a parent as that child matures.

Elizabeth, whose daughter and family were killed in a train crash, says, "My faith was so shattered that there was nothing left. I wasn't even angry with God. I just didn't believe anymore.

"Over this long journey of healing and learning, I came to believe that God doesn't make things happen, like the accident. Man-made tragedies are just that, man-made! God does support, guide, and comfort me. I wouldn't be where I am today if He hadn't been carrying me all this time. I can stand alone now, but I know He is beside me."

These spiritual questions are most often formulated during the earlier phases of grief. They deepen and become more sophisticated with time and personal growth. The answers may come later and are equally refined. Spirituality continues beyond the desolation of grief. For the Phoenix Grievers, it is a lifelong process of evolution.

Grievers breathe a sigh of relief when thinking the acute phase of grief has passed and balance is once again restored. But it is not entirely true that that the days of pain and sorrow are behind them forever.

Impact	Chaos	Adaptation	Equilibrium	Transformation

GRIEF REVISITED

It may come as a shock and surprise when a griever re-experiences some of the earlier emotional discomforts of grief, but this is to be expected. It does not mean a regression and the loss of all the growth attained. It does mean that the loved one is a part of the griever's life forever. There will be times when the absence is particularly evident, such as the birthday or death day of the loved one, or an event where the loved one should have been present. Other difficult times may be developmental passages when the loved one would have been a key figure (weddings, graduations), and events when the mourner is vulnerable and longs for the loved one's comforting presence.

> It may come as a shock and surprise when a griever re-experiences some of the earlier emotional discomforts of grief.

Paul was 20 years old when his father died. He says, "Grief is never-ending and each death opens it up again. Everyone looks for closure. They ask, when is this going to be over? There is no closure because you will miss that person for the rest of your life. Not that your life will be awful, because it will be whatever you make of it, but you will feel the absence of someone you love more deeply at certain times."

Paul expresses the feelings of many grievers. Yes, life *will* be fine, but the loved one will always be missed and, at certain times, more acutely. These brief visits back to the land of grief may be alarming. Many grievers have expressed their apprehension that they will get stuck there. The importance of understanding the normality of this phenomenon cannot be overly emphasized. It may require touching base with those who had been supportive initially. Occasionally, a mourner

| Impact | Chaos | Adaptation | Equilibrium | Transformation |

may be in a particularly vulnerable state and will need to reactivate supportive and therapeutic measures.

Phoenix Grievers came to accept the revisiting of grief. Almost always, the griever who has arrived at the point of Equilibrium, heading into Transformation, will regain the advances relatively quickly. Mourners will return from revisiting grief and resume their lives and their growth. This is important to remember because it helps to eliminate the fear that may accompany this experience. Revisiting grief is part of the process of grief.

> Revisiting grief is part of the process of grief.

THE END OF MOURNING?

Nuland (personal communication 1997), author of the acclaimed book *How We Die*, says, "Each of us carries our own grief and grief never ends. That's the one thing I'm absolutely certain of. You go through an entire lifetime and you continue to mourn what you've lost."

The Phoenix Grievers agree. Our loved ones are part of who we are and have contributed to and influenced our identities. Phoenix Grievers know that closure doesn't mean closing the door and excluding their lost loved ones from their lives. They have been forever changed by having them. And they have been forever changed by their deaths; in fact, they are far greater than they had ever expected to be.

Many grievers are quite content once they are in this phase of Equilibrium. This part of grieving brings the mitigation of pain and the familiarity of everyday life. They are enjoying their lives once again and the stability feels good. Does this mean that grief is over? Grievers have choices when they arrive at this destination. They can stay where they are or move onward. Many do not realize they have a choice. They

| Impact | Chaos | Adaptation | Equilibrium | Transformation |

are comfortable in their lives and do not choose to embark on further quests. And this is good—for them.

The Phoenix Grievers are also comfortable and balanced, yet their sights are set on distant horizons. They are inwardly restless and want more. They face forward and accept the challenges of the next phase of grief, Transformation, which is an optional exploration into unfamiliar terrain beyond the conventional boundaries of grieving.

GRIEF WORK

During the phase of Equilibrium, grievers become acclimated to the no longer strange new world and begin to achieve balance. Their self-confidence and self-esteem are well formed by the end of this phase of grief. The purpose of this phase is to design and implement a full and balanced life without the loved one, including a deepening of spirituality. In order to accomplish this, the griever must meet certain challenges.

Phoenix Grievers build and maintain equilibrium in body, mind, and spirit through creating new beliefs; letting go of self-defeating emotions such as anger, bitterness, hopelessness, and vengeance; overcoming the barrier of fear; taking risks; trying new behaviors; and learning through trial and error. Tolerating the frustration of attempting new behaviors is one of the strongest challenges. Sometimes it feels easier to remain the same, but this leads to stagnation rather than growth. The Phoenix Grievers commit themselves to being their best possible selves. They deny themselves the contentment of stopping their journeys. As many have verbalized, "It just wasn't an option! I needed to do more."

An additional challenge materializes during this phase. Grievers begin to develop an interest in a person, place, or thing. This requires a risk and making a commitment to love.

| Impact | Chaos | Adaptation | Equilibrium | Transformation |

Michelle met the challenge when she made the decision to have another child several years after little Marie died. For all the Phoenix Grievers this is one of the scariest of all steps. They realized the significance of investing their love and they did it anyway, which takes a lot of courage and a trust in the unknown. They know that life offers no guarantees.

There were many grievers who met the challenge of risking love in the latter part of Adaptation, or even later, in the phase of Transformation. It is wise to remember that many of the components of a phase may be successfully accomplished during another phase. The sequence of events is not fixed. However, the key word is *successfully*. The challenges of loving again are more completely met when grievers have moved beyond the earlier, more painful and chaotic aspects of grief.

The Phoenix Grievers, having met the challenges of this phase, offer their observations and recommendations.

FOR THE GRIEVER

- Remind yourself that anxiety and uncertainty are a normal part of this fourth phase of grief and are to be expected when facing changes and choices.
- Take time to evaluate the short- and long-term consequences of decisions. During this time of trying to balance on shaky ground, it is useful to imagine "If I do this, what will happen? If I do that what will happen?" Do what is best for you.
- Don't be afraid to admit that a decision isn't working out well. Failure is not defeat.
- Pace yourself—timing is important. Something that you're not ready for today might work very well a month from now.

| Impact | Chaos | Adaptation | Equilibrium | Transformation |

- Don't be surprised if you feel a new sense of self-awareness and stability. Some grievers have described it as the first time that they truly know and like themselves. It can even be exhilarating.
- Develop your spirituality. This is a perfect time to examine your relationship with a higher power. Work on your forgiveness issues.
- Remember that you will revisit grief periodically. Be prepared. It is not a regression. It is a *visitation*.
- Reevaluate the support system that you built earlier in the grief process. If you find that it's still helpful, by all means, stick with it. However, you may find that you have outgrown it.
- Commit yourself to balance, harmony, and a quiet simplicity of life.
- Recognize what you have accomplished so far and acknowledge your own courage and determination.
- Continue your writing or audio dialogue about your journey.
- Honor the life of your loved one by incorporating the qualities, virtues, and personality traits you have admired.
- Realize that you have passed the point of hopelessness and have balanced your life.

FOR THE THERAPIST

The therapist or other helper will be assisting the griever in the process of designing, implementing, and balancing the new lifestyle. Supporting the griever's decision making (long- and short-term) and risk taking, while monitoring his physical, emotional, and behavioral balance, is the focus. The

| Impact | Chaos | Adaptation | Equilibrium | Transformation |

griever needs validation for efforts made and growth attained. A warm, humanistic style coupled with cognitive-behavioral strategies, if necessary, is most effective during this time. Negative beliefs, although more likely to have become manifest during Adaptation, may prevent the griever from seizing the opportunities of the Phase of Equilibrium.

Table 8–1. The Phoenix Model of Grief: Equilibrium Phase

Needs	Tasks	Intervention
For:	*To:*	*Use:*
All base level needs	Maintain all previous growth	Humanistic, supportive, and less directive methods
Belonging		
Self-esteem, self-confidence	Take risks in developing new relationships and roles	Humanistic, supportive, and less directive methods
	Achieve and maintain balance	Cognitive-behavioral techniques for negative beliefs
Considering self-actualization	Consider developing self-potential and moving toward self-actualization	Encouragement in supporting the potential for Transformation
		Develop proactive strategies for "grief revisited"

It is especially helpful if the therapist has some experience with the role of spirituality in the treatment of grief. It is not unusual for a griever's spiritual quest to influence or challenge the therapist's own. If the therapist is not comfortable

Impact	Chaos	Adaptation	Equilibrium	Transformation

or has a limited spiritual comfort zone, it is wise to refer the griever to a spiritual advisor.

Therapists may not see grievers during the latter parts of the Equilibrium phase. The acute pain is over, life has stabilized and balanced, and the griever may not be experiencing any distress. Grievers may consult their therapists when they "revisit grief," or when another serious loss causes acute symptoms to resurface. They may cycle back to the beginning phases of grief, signaling the need for brief therapy. Here are some guidelines for therapists to consider.

- **Listen:** Identify where in Equilibrium the griever is. Earlier involvement needs more support. Remember, the griever could be experiencing "grief revisited."
- **Normalize:** Explain the process if the person has cycled back to an acute phase of grief. Better still, discuss the symptoms of "grief revisited" before the griever leaves therapy. Be proactive and informative.
- **Assess:** Evaluate the griever's needs according to the Phoenix Model.
- **Plan:** Co-design a plan to achieve or restore homeostasis. Refer the griever for augmentative therapy, if necessary, such as medication, a spiritual advisor, or a career counselor.
- **Intervene:** Prioritize treatment according to the assessment. Equilibrium is the goal.
- **Support:** Assist the griever's plans toward that goal.
- **Educate:** Orientate the griever to where she is in the grief process and what personal danger signs might manifest. Empower through knowledge.
- **Monitor:** Be alert for complications or regressions. Initiate treatment at once if necessary.

| Impact | Chaos | Adaptation | Equilibrium | Transformation |

SUMMARY

- The phase of Equilibrium is both challenging and exciting.
- Grievers commit to developing a life without the loved one.
- Their lives attain balance and harmony later in this phase.
- The pain of grief surfaces only periodically when "grief is revisited," during special times when the loved one's absence is particularly painful.
- The grievers' lives have, once again, achieved balance.
- Phoenix Grievers move beyond this phase to assist others through the growth they have attained.

And it came to pass that the group of grievers bade farewell to their guides. It was time to return to their village. It was a homecoming of a different sort for a few of the grievers. . . .

| Impact | Chaos | Adaptation | Equilibrium | Transformation |

9

The Phoenix Soars: Phase Five—Transformation

And some of the grievers returned to their village to carry on with their lives. The others paused to reflect on their experiences through grief. . . .

Transformation is optional. It is not for everyone. But for those who choose to extend and expand their growth its rewards are boundless. The grievers' lives have stabilized at a new and orderly pace. The script has changed, as have some of the actors, but the Phoenix Griever is now the director.

Transformation, like Maslow's self-actualization, leads grievers beyond the familiar territory to new opportunities and a variety of settings for spiritual alchemy. Altruism blossoms in this phase. During this time, the Phoenix Griever becomes conscious of his growth and feels profound gratitude and appreciation. He also recognizes his own part in achieving it and its gifts.

According to Bess and Bartlett (1974), "Creative grief might be considered . . . as a reflection of an abiding love for the deceased" (p. 317). In other words, those who use their grieving toward something beneficial honor their loved ones. Phoenix Grievers are those who go beyond the accustomed

| Impact | Chaos | Adaptation | Equilibrium | Transformation |

work of mourning, who bring into being something of value, for themselves
and for others. They are more than
life's survivors; they are life's champi-
ons.

> Phoenix Grievers . . .
> are more than life's
> survivors; they are
> life's champions.

SELF-ACTUALIZATION

Maslow's (1987) term *self-actualization*
describes "people who have developed or
are developing into the full stature of
which they are capable" (p. 126). Note
that he uses the verb "developing."
These individuals do not just stop where
they are. They continue to learn, grow,
create, and help others.

> **Phase Five**
> *Transformation*
> Self-Actualization
> Awareness
> Renaissance
> Compassion
> Creating Meaning
> Acquiring Purpose
> Altruism
> The Legacy

Phoenix Grievers are also moved by
a curiosity to want to learn more about
themselves, others, and the world in
general. They gravitate toward situations that provide new
understanding about life. It is not unusual to find them in
either formal or informal classrooms as students or teachers.
In this manner they continue their lifelong growth in giving
and receiving knowledge.

Hope, whose son committed suicide, returned to college to
further her nursing profession. "At first I needed to understand
everything about suicide. As I continued, my purpose changed.
I needed to grow and learn for me, so that I could help others
who were in physical or emotional pain."

Creating meaning and establishing a direction and purpose
in life are continual goals for the Phoenix Grievers as they

| Impact | Chaos | Adaptation | Equilibrium | Transformation |

continue their journeys through life. The deaths of their loved ones started them on a passage of evolution toward enlightenment. Their journeys, which originated in pain and darkness, have resulted in illumination and well-being. Phoenix Grievers and their odysseys are ongoing works-in-progress.

AWARENESS

While mindful of their growth and appreciative of what life has to offer them, Phoenix Grievers remain matter-of-fact about their perseverance ("What else could I do?"). They do not consider themselves extraordinary even though they have triumphed over unimaginable crises.

Elizabeth, bereaved mother and grandmother, states her feelings succinctly: "There are only two choices: go on, survive and live, or quit, give up, and die. Number two was not an option for me."

Phoenix Grievers have acknowledged that there were times when they thought of quitting, but they didn't entertain the thought for long. If the feelings lingered, they sought professional help. In other words, they took responsibility for their lives and refused to be victims.

Although Phoenix Grievers appreciate the "gifts" of their struggles they are also saddened by the circumstances that led to their forced metamorphoses. Their ambivalence is not unusual.

Elizabeth clarifies this viewpoint: "Sometimes, my appreciation of life is a bittersweet reward. Not so much a feeling of guilt, but part of an oppressive sadness for not being able to share it with my absent loved ones."

Impact	Chaos	Adaptation	Equilibrium	Transformation

Stephanie, whose future husband, Davis, was murdered, says, "I wouldn't be where I am today if I hadn't gone through this crisis. I wouldn't be who I am without knowing Davis. It's so sad that I am this healthy and happy for the first time in my life and he who helped me get here isn't here to enjoy it."

Many grievers share the "what might have been" perspective. They continue to acknowledge and include their loved ones in their minds, hearts, and souls.

Phoenix Grievers also question whether growth and maturity can be achieved without the struggles. Perhaps they cannot. According to psychiatrist and author, Dr. Ned Cassem (1975): "Tragedy and adversity have often challenged, activated or highlighted the loftiest sentiments and behavior in human history. . . . The person grows in spite of the loss or disaster" (p. 9). A bereaved mother expresses the duality of her feelings. "I wouldn't have asked for this, but I am profoundly grateful for who I am now—someone I would not have dreamed I could be."

The Phoenix Grievers are deeply aware of the impermanence and unpredictability of this life. After all, they have felt the impact of life's capriciousness. Conversely, the imperfections of the human condition have released them from their former absolute standards. One formerly perfectionist widow says, "Life is imperfect and so are we. I eased up on my expectations of myself and others."

The long road to Transformation has been filled with wounds, pain, and scars. The Phoenix Grievers needed stamina, determination, and courage to transcend the throes of grief. Each obstacle they faced, each challenge they met, added to their strengths. Whatever dormant resources were in them they brought forth and learned to use. Their emergent proficiencies have been well earned.

Impact	Chaos	Adaptation	Equilibrium	Transformation

Michelle, who faced several challenges of loss, eloquently states: "I am not proud of the wounds I suffered when my children died, but . . . I am very proud of the scars!"

> "I am not proud of the wounds I suffered when my children died, but . . . I am very proud of the scars."

This simple message has profound implications for others. Life brings wounds and it is our responsibility to develop scars that strengthen the whole person.

Phoenix Grievers concur that gratitude emerges as a strong component of their lives. "Significant losses often serve as turning points in people's lives and lead to new perspectives on the meaning of what is important in living" (Benoliel 1985, p. 233). What may have been taken for granted is now more valued. Life itself is more appreciated.

The sequential deaths of her husband, father, and fiancé could have left Megan cynical and bitter. She comments on this: "You might say I have learned what is important and what isn't and this truly guides my path in life. I appreciate what life has to offer. I miss what is not here, but I am grateful for what is."

Dianna, whose daughter Grace died, says, "I am very aware of how beautiful life is so I enjoy much more in it. I am appreciative of the smallest things. I no longer assume my loved ones will always be there so I am grateful for the time I am with them."

Whereas initially the Phoenix Grievers did not feel they could cope with the presenting loss, they are now aware that they had exactly what they needed all along. They often compare themselves with others and realize they could be much worse off; their tragedies have been more manageable than those of others. "I don't know how she can do it," says one widow of another's grief. They add empathy to the attributes of their renaissance.

| Impact | Chaos | Adaptation | Equilibrium | Transformation |

RENAISSANCE

This state of rebirth or revival blends all the resources that were originally parts of the grievers' personalities with the strengths developed during their grieving experiences. Eisenstadt (1978) describes the process leading up to it: "In the creative mourning process, there is a sequence of events whereby the loss triggers off a crisis requiring mastery on the part of the bereaved individual. If this crisis is worked through, that is, if the destructive elements and the depressive features of the experience of bereavement are neutralized, then a creative product or a creatively integrated personality can result" (p. 220).

Phoenix Grievers consider what might have been if their grief had a different outcome.

David, whose daughter was murdered, ponders the outcome of his grieving process. "If I hadn't shared with others and worked with the prisoners, then life would have little meaning. I would probably spend my life judging and criticizing others."

Michelle relates her personal feelings about her renaissance: "Making the choice to grow, rather than staying stuck in self-pity, rage, and despair, gives meaning to their short lives. I see that much of who I am is the result of gifts of my daughters. I think they are proud of me."

Does self-actualization mean that these exceptional grievers are saints and live an idyllic life? Is there a dark side to their luster? Maslow (1968) says: "Self-actualization does not mean a transcendence of all human problems. Conflicts, anxiety, frustration, sadness, hurt and guilt can all be found in healthy human beings" (p. 210).

Mark, husband of Michelle and father of little Marie, interprets this statement on a personal level: "I would like to say that I look

Impact	Chaos	Adaptation	Equilibrium	Transformation

at every day as a gift. Well, there are days I don't. There are times I get caught up with work, to the sacrifice of my family. But those are little steps backward in the big picture. My emphasis is to look positively to the future and to my family."

Mark describes how easy it is for anyone to lose perspective on hard-won values when faced by the tribulations of daily life. Our fast-paced society sweeps us up into its vortex and sometimes sheer survival is all we can manage. However, these exceptional people get back on track very quickly. They don't stay stuck for long. Their commitment is to maintain and improve on their growth and maturity.

Phoenix Grievers sheepishly admit to working on an intolerance of people who whine. They are more than willing to help those who want to help themselves, but lack patience with those who only complain. This is not an uncommon attitude. Siebert (1996) says, "Most people with positive attitudes have a negative attitude about people with negative attitudes" (p. 111). And he offers this perspective: "Negative people give you an opportunity to practice being flexible, playful, empathic and synergistic" (p. 116).

Life presents myriad chances to strengthen our coping, adaptation, and growth skills. If grievers recognize that frustration and conflict present opportunities to bring forth a higher-level response, they may be more motivated to do so.

Phoenix Grievers were candid in revealing areas where they feel they took a little longer to grow. For many, one such area was dealing with the risk of loving again. All too aware of the fragility of life, they expressed apprehension about losing another loved one. Over time, they worked on eliminating the barriers of fear in order to love again because they felt that love was a necessary ingredient for their quality of life.

Impact	Chaos	Adaptation	Equilibrium	Transformation

Michelle, bereaved mother, learned that "Love is the most important emotion of all. It is the real reason we are all here, to love and to love well. No matter how much it hurts when that beloved is gone, the imprint and memory of love is always with us. The love never dies."

When Phoenix Grievers discussed their growth and change, the concept of love came up time and time again as the number one gift from their adversities.

During renaissance Phoenix Grievers see themselves in a different way. Calhoun and Tedeschi (1989–1990), in a study with bereaved individuals, showed that "The most prevalent and perhaps most important positive changes reported were in the area of self-perception" (p. 269). Their respondents, like the Phoenix Grievers, described themselves as "stronger or more competent persons in several ways including the following: more mature, more independent, better able to face other crises and changed into a stronger or wiser person" (p. 269).

Maggie, whose husband died after a protracted illness, believes that "I am more independent and my identity is my own and not a reflection of someone else's."

Noella, who was left with two children to raise, says, "I know I am a better person today for having lived through this. I'm very capable of caring for myself as well as others."

Megan, who lost her husband, her father, and her fiancé, says, "I am wiser and stronger now. Each death prepared me for the next. All of them made me a better person."

Karin and Stuart had been married for five years when he was killed in an automobile accident. She says, "I felt I was shattered

| Impact | Chaos | Adaptation | Equilibrium | Transformation |

into pieces after the loss. This tragedy gave me new ways to put my pieces together to increase my learning, growth, and compassion."

> "This tragedy gave me new ways to put my pieces together to increase my learning, growth, and compassion."

The renaissance reflected a tapestry of interwoven strands. Each Phoenix Griever entered the grieving process at a different level of interpersonal growth with distinct skills, resources, and talents. Strengths became stronger. Potentials emerged. After the death of his son, Rabbi Harold Kushner wrote: "I am a more sensitive person, a more effective pastor, a more sympathetic counselor because of Aaron's life and death than I would ever have been without it" (1981, p. 133).

Rabbi Kushner describes becoming "more" than he was before the death of his son. Phoenix Grievers report the same expansion of their personalities as well as the development of new aspects. Those who were pessimists became optimists, the meek became bold, the passive, assertive, the closed, open, the judgmental, forgiving, the unappreciative, grateful. For Phoenix Grievers, growth was not merely an expansion of formerly held virtues, but the emergence of new buds on the existent tree.

Julian, whose brother Vince died in a skiing accident, believes he is different in many ways since his loss. He explains: "I am unconventional where I was conservative and have taken charge over my own life rather than live the expected plan for me. It is still hard for me to explain the paradox of becoming a risk taker as a result of my brother taking too great a risk. I suppose we need to achieve balance in life."

David, whose daughter was murdered, has added new dimensions to his personality. "I am open with my thoughts and feel-

Impact	Chaos	Adaptation	Equilibrium	Transformation

ings, I reach out to others, I am self-directed and follow through on what I believe to be right for me and for others. I am not afraid to help those in need. I was not this way before her death."

Rae Ann, who donated the organs of her daughter Kayla, killed in a motor vehicle accident, describes an amalgam of changes in her personality. She says: "I have changed A LOT. I am more introspective, calmer, enjoy solitude, no longer afraid of death, more open to experiences that have no physical evidence [supernatural], more accepting of others and especially of myself."

Rae Ann remarks on not being afraid of death anymore. This is a frequent commentary from the Phoenix Grievers. Somewhere in the process of grief they have arrived at a spiritual peace in their lives and in contemplation of their deaths. With this comes a relative degree of comfort with the whereabouts of their loved ones in an afterlife. And the resolution is reciprocal. Once the grievers feel that the spirit of their loved one lives on, the concept of death is no longer frightening.

Early in this phase Phoenix Grievers reflect on the experiences that have contributed to the development of new and positive aspects of themselves. They agree that their personal tragedies have given them strengths that would have taken many years to develop, if they ever did.

Ann was 14 years old when her mother died. "I wouldn't be the person I am today. I'm better for having gone through it. I wouldn't be as self-sufficient and confident as I am."

Megan feels that the experiences of her triple loss "have made me a stronger person. I am more self-aware of my capabilities to love and understand others, face my fears and limitations. I

| Impact | Chaos | Adaptation | Equilibrium | Transformation |

am able to put stressful and emotional situations in perspective and I no longer overreact to them."

Maggie reflects on her changes: "I am doing things I never thought I would or even could. I look at events and people in a different way now. I choose those that add to my emotional and spiritual maturity as I continue my journey."

In the words of Dean Koontz (1996): "Only the human spirit can act with volition and consciously change itself; it is the only thing in all creation that is not entirely at the mercy of forces outside itself, and it is, therefore, the most powerful and valuable form of energy in the universe."

COMPASSION

Every Phoenix Griever reported being much more compassionate than ever before. They choose this descriptive word over and over as they describe their transformations. It encompasses not only an awareness but also an understanding of another's pain, and further, a willingness to relieve it.

Amy, whose twin brother Jeffrey died, says, "Before he died, I had no idea what going through grief meant. Now I extend myself to help others who have lost siblings. I know what they're feeling, I know how to help and I go out of my way to be there for them."

Stephanie, whose future husband was murdered, says, "I am so much more compassionate in the way I look at others. I believe in giving everyone a chance and looking past superficialities to find the diamonds in the rough. I look beyond what used to be my prejudices. They no longer exist. I have a way of looking at the essence of a person now."

Impact	Chaos	Adaptation	Equilibrium	Transformation

Phoenix Grievers are cognizant that pain is part of this journey through life and they know that something good can come out of it. They can see beyond the pain. They view it in a larger context.

Michelle says, "I feel that I now have the courage and compassion to be present for those in psychological, physical, and spiritual pain. I can be there for someone without letting it consume or overwhelm me. I have enough to share."

It would seem that Phoenix Grievers' hearts have increased in their capacity for compassion. Indeed, the bounty they have accumulated during their own experiential journey has become a source of beneficence toward others. Compassion acts as a catalyst for the transformative experiences of creating meaning, acquiring purpose, and expressing altruism.

CREATING MEANING

Searching for a meaning in a meaningless event challenges every person who has ever lost a loved one. Kushner (1981) says, "We can redeem these tragedies from senselessness by imposing meaning on them. The question we should be asking is not 'Why did this happen to me?' . . . A better question would be 'Now that this has happened to me, what am I going to do about it?' " (p. 136).

> Searching for a meaning in a meaningless event challenges every person who has ever lost a loved one.

Nuland (1997), whose mother died when he was 11 years old, says, "Life has only the meaning we find in it and . . . we have to use every opportunity to look for [it]. To find meaning is our salvation" (personal communication).

| Impact | Chaos | Adaptation | Equilibrium | Transformation |

People can endure almost anything if they can find meaning in it. The Phoenix Grievers are no different in that sense. They refused to allow their loved ones' lives and deaths to be without meaning. It was up to them to be the architects and contractors for their constructions of meaning.

Each griever ultimately owns the responsibility for creating meaning from the life and the death of a loved one. And each Phoenix Griever demonstrates this creativity differently.

Noella decided to go back to school. She became a teacher and was able to improve the quality of life for herself and her sons. She realized that she needed to do more. She says, "I needed to create something meaningful from Bob's death and from my experience through grief. I needed to make a difference in others' lives, especially those in crisis. I returned to school and became a therapist. This gave me a new purpose, to create meaning from the tragedy."

Joyce, whose daughter and husband died, was also motivated to help others. She did so, gradually. She states, "Their deaths have been such tremendous losses that I cannot allow them to have no meaning. It [death] must produce something of meaning or it becomes totally pointless."

> "Their deaths have been such tremendous losses that I cannot allow them to have no meaning. It [death] must produce something of meaning or it becomes totally pointless."

Becoming stronger, wiser, and more compassionate, Joyce channeled her energy into becoming a professional woman. Through her expanded self she was able to help others through her work and as a volunteer, both regionally and nationally, in The Compassionate Friends Society. She held

| Impact | Chaos | Adaptation | Equilibrium | Transformation |

both the conviction and the commitment requisite to a meaningful outcome.

Phoenix Grievers are motivated toward creating meaning for various reasons. Many are influenced by their beliefs.

Karin, whose husband Stuart was killed in an automobile crash, says, "I believe there is a reason for this happening. My belief system tells me: 'because you can do something with it.'"

Karin believes that there is a personal meaning for her in this tragedy. She knows that she has the necessary abilities to do something that will ultimately produce something meaningful from the death of her young husband.

Stephanie, whose future husband was murdered, explains, "If I didn't turn this around and make something positive, then I have lost an opportunity to grow. If I don't find something good in this, then he died in vain."

Phoenix Grievers transform their tragedies into triumphs of magnanimity, and through their desire to help others, they receive more than they could imagine.

It is important to note that most Phoenix Grievers had reached the stability of Equilibrium before they had energy to share. Most of them needed to stabilize themselves first before they were able to extend themselves in an altruistic way.

Michelle wanted to "do something to help others and lessen the initial pain. I wanted to create something meaningful, right away. It was too soon. It took me a long time before I was upright and stable enough to give of myself to others. I learned this after creating more chaos and exhaustion by reaching out to help, rather than reaching out to receive help."

| Impact | Chaos | Adaptation | Equilibrium | Transformation |

Maggie says, "I am a born caregiver and continued this throughout my adult life. I have a great need to give of myself. I am much more vigilant about receiving now. I also need to receive that ripple effect back."

Creating meaning from a loved one's death comes from strength and abundance, which take time. And timing counts. The desire to help others may exist during earlier phases; however, the energy does not.

Attention to the self as well as to others is essential for balanced grieving.

On initial perception, a tragedy appears to be devoid of creative opportunity. It is only with the passage of time that the potential is revealed. Over time, like Rumpelstiltskin, the griever "spins straw into gold," through the process of spiritual alchemy.

> Over time, like Rumpelstiltskin, the griever "spins straw into gold. . . ."

Siebert (1998) offers this observation about grievers helping grievers: "Creating meaning from death can also apply to the grief process itself. When survivors speak out, they must go back and relive the experience, albeit on a different level, with a sense of perspective. They no longer feel emotionally wounded when their minds go back. Thus, they are able to willingly help others so that what they went through has meaning and purpose" (personal communication).

A PURPOSE IN LIFE

A purpose in life is a set of beliefs about what best reflects the inner self as it interacts with the external world. It develops from the intention to create something fruitful from something fallow. And it propels a griever toward a benefi-

| Impact | Chaos | Adaptation | Equilibrium | Transformation |

cial outcome or process. When this purpose comes to life, it does so through attitude and behavior.

Stephanie, whose future husband was murdered, says, "My purpose is to grow and present an example of courage. I need to give the message to others, 'you can transcend anything.' "

Many Phoenix Grievers feel that their grief helps them design a blueprint for life. Purpose and direction can originate in the stages of Adaptation and Equilibrium, but emerge most intensely in the phase of Transformation. Examples of earlier onsets are Noella and Joyce, who began their education during Adaptation, and Michelle, who slowly began working toward her profession in child psychology in late Adaptation. Karin was in graduate school when Stuart was killed; she continued on to pursue her doctorate in clinical psychology. Some of them recognized the opportunity in tragedy and discovered their purposes still earlier during the phase of Impact. Many asked themselves, "What would my loved one have expected of me?" Their answers helped define purpose and direction in life.

> Many asked themselves, "What would my loved one have expected of me?"

Emma, who lost several children, kept her purpose in mind, even after each loss. She explains: "I knew what they would have wanted me to do. This gave me the determination to find the way and the strength to go forward. I was to live my life fully and help others with their grief."

Elizabeth, left with a grandchild to raise when the family was killed in a crash, knew immediately what her purpose was to be. "I will help to raise this child of my beloved daughter. I will do what she would have wanted me to do. I have a purpose and that is to bring him up in the way she would have wanted."

| Impact | Chaos | Adaptation | Equilibrium | Transformation |

Ann, whose mother died when she was 14, knew what was expected of her. Her purpose was clear. "My purpose is to make her (my mother) proud of me, wherever she is. It keeps me going in the right direction. I know that doing the best I can do, at everything, will make her proud."

Gordon Allport (1969) made this statement about purpose in life: "No man can tell another what this purpose is. Each must find out for himself, and must accept the responsibility for what this purpose is. If he succeeds he will continue to grow in spite of all indignities" (p. xiii). The Phoenix Grievers are living examples of his words.

Occasionally, grievers learn from their loved ones' lack of purpose, like Scott, who was able to neutralize and alchemize the tragedy of his father's life and death.

The suicide of Scott's father reversed his objectives in life. He says, "More than anything I vowed that I would not waste my life and its opportunities the way he did. I would do what he could not, live cleanly [without substances], live honestly, and live meaningfully. These were my purposes; the destination would come later."

Today, Scott is a state police officer, with some commendations to his credit.

With purpose giving them a direction, Phoenix Grievers develop the urge to share their gifts and lessons with other people. Enter altruism.

ALTRUISM

"Altruism is never truly unselfish. I believe that we personally benefit from helping others. It feels good and it increases

| Impact | Chaos | Adaptation | Equilibrium | Transformation |

our self-esteem" (Siebert 1998). Phoenix Grievers confirm that
they have received more than they have given.

Carole, the physician, says, "Grief is like
mathematics. It can add, subtract, or multi-
ply what you have in your soul. Giving to
others, helping others in their need and pain
multiplies goodness into the world and increases the treasures in your soul."

> "Grief is like
> mathematics. It
> can add, subtract,
> or multiply what
> you have in your
> soul."

Bess and Bartlett (1974) said, "In whatever form it may
appear, the outlet for our sorrow often may lie in ministry to
the wider needs of the world or in the unending battle against
injustices. A world marked by such needs offers many sav-
ing outlets to those who must ask, Where do I use the passion of my grief?" (p. 318).

Phoenix Grievers find ways to use the passion of their grief.
By their very presence, through teaching and sharing their
experiences, by becoming involved in causes that benefit others, by giving their time and/or money, Phoenix Grievers all
find ways to make a difference in others' lives. Some Phoenix Grievers have founded national and international organizations to support or prevent others' grief, such as Compassionate Friends Society (an international organization for
parents who have lost children) and M.A.D.D. (Mothers
Against Drunk Driving).

Joyce, whose daughter and husband died, describes her altruism: "I am strongly committed to creating a meaningful life for
myself. I searched for a way to serve others that nourishes me
at the same time. I found it in the Compassionate Friends Society. I volunteer my time and energy on both a local and national
level."

Impact	Chaos	Adaptation	Equilibrium	Transformation

David, whose daughter was murdered, says, "God has used my wounds as well as my gifts to reach out to others and in the process has helped me to heal. I certainly did not get involved in prison ministry in order to be healed—that is simply a happy by-product."

Through their spiritual alchemy and altruism, Phoenix Grievers do receive something in return. They continue to offer the world living legacies of their loved ones.

THE LEGACY

History is crowded with legacies, both good and bad, that have followed the deaths of loved ones. Judith Viorst (1986) speaks of the legacy of identification when someone beloved dies. She says, "It is through identifications that we can develop and enrich our emerging self. And through identifications, we can take into ourselves aspects of those we have loved and lost— aspects that are often abstract but are on occasion startlingly concrete. . . . By taking in the dead—by making them part of what we think, feel, love, want, do—we can both keep them with us and let them go" (p. 249).

Each person leaves something of himself when he leaves this life. In this way, the spirit of who he was lives on. Dean Koontz (1996) summarizes: "We need only choose . . . by the way we live [to] celebrate . . . those who loved us and who were loved."

GRIEF WORK

Once Equilibrium has been established, all grievers have an opportunity to further their growth by developing their unique

| Impact | Chaos | Adaptation | Equilibrium | Transformation |

potential toward a greater goal. These are the purposes of the phase of Transformation. Grievers must identify their unique life purposes and head steadily in that direction. They have opportunities to alchemize their unredeeming tragedies into triumphant testimonies to the human capacity for transcendence.

FOR THE GRIEVER

Phoenix Grievers suggest:

- Reflect back on what you were like before the death of your loved one. Identify how you have changed. Give thanks.
- Look for ways to create meaning from what you have been through.
- Look for your own special purpose in life and head in that direction.
- Find a way to share your gifts by helping others.
- Live your life so that your loved one has not died in vain. Bring honor to that person's life.
- Become a living legacy of your loved one.

FOR THE THERAPIST

In their offices therapists are least likely to see people engaged in Transformation. Consider yourself very lucky if you do. It is a privilege to work with them and learn from them. They exemplify a level of human development that is very rare indeed.

　　There are Phoenix Grievers who choose to continue their growth in partnership with a therapist. Others may seek a therapeutic ear if a crisis occurs in their lives, especially if

| Impact | Chaos | Adaptation | Equilibrium | Transformation |

they have benefited from it previously. Therapists' roles should adapt to the needs and tasks of the Phoenix Model of bereavement. Phoenix Grievers themselves will be familiar with the process. Guide them through.

Of course, therapists should be on the alert for any additional compromising circumstances, any concurrent situational or developmental life crises. These may include divorce, medical problems, further losses, geographical relocation, or other stressors that would impinge on the grief process. They should be factored into the treatment plan and may lengthen and/or intensify the course of therapy. Phoenix Grievers who have reached the phase of Transformation will most often return to it.

Table 9-1. The Phoenix Model of Grief: Transformation Phase

Needs	Tasks	Intervention
For:	*To:*	*Use:*
All previous level needs	Maintain all previous growth	Crisis intervention and/or other brief psychotherapeutic modalities for additional life crises or "grief revisited"
Recognizing and fulfilling one's unique potential	Create meaning from the life and death of the loved one and the grief experience	Humanistic, supportive techniques; little need for directive measures unless asked
Self-actualization	Pursue purpose in life	Willingness to learn from Phoenix Grievers
	Share gifts of wisdom, time, and energy through altruistic pursuits. Further develop potential	

| Impact | Chaos | Adaptation | Equilibrium | Transformation |

SUMMARY

- The phase of Transformation is characterized by awareness, acknowledgment, and gratitude for growth.
- Phoenix Grievers integrate the admired qualities of
  their loved ones with those they developed during the
  process of grieving.
- They reach out to make a difference in others' lives
  through spiritual alchemy and through the way they live
  their own lives.
- The legacy of their deceased loved ones is love, compassion, deeper spirituality, and altruism.
- They continue to grow throughout their lives.
- The lives and deaths of their loved ones continue to
  affect the world in a loving way.

**And it came to pass that they chose to return whence
they began—at the dwelling place of The Wise One. . . .**

| Impact | Chaos | Adaptation | Equilibrium | Transformation |

10

Legacy of the Phoenix

And the Wise One welcomed them back from their journey and wondered how they would use their wisdom and gifts.

THE LESSONS

The Phoenix Grievers have traveled through darkness, pain, and despair, emerging into a place of abundance and hope. Through meeting the challenges of their experiences, they have earned a bounty of gifts and assimilated decades of wisdom in an accelerated course on life. Inasmuch as one of their gifts is altruism, the Phoenix Grievers willingly and graciously share what they have learned. Therapists might find it helpful sharing the recommendations with grievers.

LESSON 1: Learn everything you can about grief.

Why:

- Every loss you have ever experienced contains some of the elements of grief, although not of the magnitude or intensity associated with the loss of a loved one.
- Every loss has recognizable elements such as sorrow, loneliness, fear, anxiety, and physical disturbances.

- You can re-use the responses you have used to cope with adversity in the past, the ones that have been healthy for you and you will learn new ones.
- Familiarizing yourself with the process of grief will help you to understand what is happening and what you can do about it. It will offer you a step-by-step guide.

How:

- Seek out the many excellent books on grief at the library or bookstores. Many self-help groups have their own libraries for grievers to use.
- Find other grievers whom you believe to be positive role models.
- Therapists, clergy, and funeral directors are other sources of information.
- Attend a workshop or course on grief when you are ready.

When:

- Most grievers find themselves researching grief when they are in its midst.
- During Chaos and Adaptation, after the shock of Impact has worn off, grievers seek and receive information.
- During Equilibrium and Transformation, Phoenix Grievers give information.

LESSON 2: Honor your grief.

Why:

- Your grief is a direct response to the depth of the love and attachment to your loved one. In some ways, you might say it is a testimony to having loved.
- It offers a way to integrate all that your loved one has meant to you.

- It presents a time frame in which to incorporate yesterday's memories into today and today's into tomorrow through rituals and remembering.
- Grief is a bridge to your future over which you will carry the legacy of your loved one.

How:

- Through organ donation.
- Through rituals that celebrate the loved one's life.
- Through memorials, scholarships, works of art, music, and writing.
- Through incorporating the deceased's admired qualities into your personality.
- Through embracing the loved one's mission or passion in life.
- Through the spiritual alchemy of altruism.

When:

- Through organ donation and fund allocation during Impact.
- Through minimal efforts during Chaos.
- Through tangible or symbolic and some altruistic expression during Adaptation and Equilibrium.
- Through all creative expression during Transformation, as a living legacy.

LESSON 3: Express your grief.

Why:

- This is one of the most important lessons. Grief contained is toxic to the mind, body, and spirit.
- Its expression and expulsion are necessary for cleansing and healing the wounds of loss.
- Grief is a natural and adaptive process.

- Grief contains steps toward adaptation, healing, and growth.

How:

- Through *verbal* expression: talking it out with a trusted person or group, audio-taping your pain, "talking" with deceased loved ones at the cemetery or elsewhere, singing, screaming, crying.
- Through *creative* expression: writing, drawing, painting, crafts, baking, gardening.
- Through *bodily* expression: exercise, yoga, massage.
- Through *listening* to others: other grievers, members of support groups, a therapist, doctor, clergy, family, friends.
- Through *self-soothing*: meditation, yoga, prayer, music.
- Through *sharing* with others whatever you have to offer: time, energy, expertise, comfort. Set aside a brief time, daily, to grieve. Get your pain out!

When:

- It is vital during the first three phases of grief: Impact, Chaos, and Adaptation.
- It becomes intermittent and episodic during Equilibrium and Transformation.
- It may not surface during the latter two phases, Equilibrium and Transformation, unless grief is revisited or another crisis of loss emerges. Then it may erupt with considerable force.

LESSON 4: Stabilize your body and your environment.

Why:

- Nothing can be built on a shaky foundation—not a house, not a reconstructed life. Think of grieving as a process of constructing a house. The foundation has to be in place and solid before the next level can be placed over it.

- Grief is a powerful force and your body must be prepared. Your physical needs will be the most important to fill. Then you need to provide some structure in your life.
- Restoring some order out of Chaos assists you in decreasing your anxiety and fear. It helps to experience something familiar.

How:

- Through feeding and nurturing your body in healthy ways: good food, exercise, rest, sleep.
- Through connecting to your health team.
- Through simplifying your routine; eliminating unnecessary "shoulds."
- Through emotional and physical expressions of pain.
- Through saying "no" to further stress and saying "yes" to help.

When:

- It is critical during the first two phases of grief, Impact and Chaos. It forms the foundation for living without the loved one.
- It must be maintained during all the rest of the phases of grief.
- It may emerge as a dominant need during grief revisited.

LESSON 5: Connect to others.

Why:

- Historically, people gather to help and support others in times of crisis and need.

- People provide practical support as well as emotional comfort and guidance.
- They provide structure and order, temporarily, when your world is fractured.
- They protect against isolation and alienation.
- Those who are role models in grief provide a vision of the future and assistance along the path.

How:

- Through asking for and accepting assistance from trusted family members, friends, neighbors, Phoenix Grievers, support groups, clergy, therapists, co-workers.
- Through allowing others to be with you.

When:

- During the first three phases of grief, it makes sense to receive as much assistance, support, and guidance as possible.
- Somewhere toward the end of Adaptation and the beginning of Equilibrium, the pendulum swings. Then you, the griever, are in a position to give to others. The connective bonds shift.

LESSON 6: Watch for your personal danger signs.

Why:

- Grief calls on every coping mechanism and strength you have available. Not all may be healthy.
- The pseudo-relief that comes from substance abuse can be dangerously seductive.
- Depression masks your ability to assess yourself.
- Rage can explode like an overheated pressure cooker.
- Illness may develop.

- All symptoms can catch you off-guard. Proactive measures should be in place to prevent maladaptive grieving.

How:

- Pay attention to your early warning signs.
- Ask your friends and family members to be your personal "watchdogs."
- Listen to their concerns and follow through with a restorative plan.
- See your family physician at the first sign of trouble.
- Ask for advice from a helping professional or support group.
- Find a role model such as a Phoenix Griever to act as your personal sponsor.

When:

- This is critical during the first three phases of grief.
- It may be necessary with the occurrence of grief revisited or if another loss or crisis situation occurs during phases of Equilibrium and Transformation.

LESSON 7: Confront and redesign your beliefs.

Why:

- Your beliefs are going to affect how you think, feel, and act.
- Your past beliefs worked with your past experiences. However, new information was presented when your loved one died.
- Your beliefs about life, death, and your ability to cope may need to be re-examined and redesigned.

How:

- Through identifying your past and present beliefs.
- Through examining which ones work for you now.
- Through confronting those that do not.
- Through self-talk and self-coaching methods.
- Through therapy.
- Through learning about cognitive-behavioral techniques.

When:

- It is crucial during the phases of Chaos and Adaptation.
- It is sporadic during Equilibrium.
- It becomes optional during Transformation. Sometimes a tune-up is necessary.

LESSON 8: Make a commitment to life.

Why:

- If you don't know what you are committed to, how will you choose the best strategies toward a goal?
- Your commitment assures that there be no further losses from the death of your loved one.
- It forces you to make the healthiest and most adaptive choices for living.
- It provides you with purpose and direction.
- It allows you to develop your potential—who you are and what you are capable of becoming.
- It brings forth the best of you to share with others.

How:

- Strengthen your foundation—your body and environment.
- Connect to others. Reach out for help, a support network.

- Establish small goals toward living.
- Believe in yourself and your abilities to navigate the passages of grief.
- Think of what your loved one would want for you.
- Never, ever give up hope.

When:

- It manifests minimally during Impact and Chaos.
- It becomes stronger during Adaptation.
- It is active during Equilibrium.
- It is a fait accompli during Transformation.

LESSON 9: Create or recreate your spirituality.

Why:

- You are more than your physical body. It is merely the spacesuit in which your spirit navigates this earth.
- You are here to develop who you are.
- You have choices and opportunities for growth.
- You are connected to a higher spirit whom you have interpreted from your spiritual developmental level.
- Faith is how you "prove" your spiritual beliefs.
- Faith is one of the most powerful of all your resources.

How:

- Listen to your inner questioning.
- Learn about different spiritual viewpoints.
- Attend rituals of worship until you connect with one.
- Write about your spiritual quest.
- Meditate and pray.
- Find a spiritual advisor.
- Clear the excess baggage from your soul to make room for your spirituality.

- Get rid of the anger, resentment, self-pity, envy, intolerance, prejudice—anything that is taking up space and paying no rent.
- Work on forgiveness.
- Keep the lines of communication open with your higher spirit.

When:

- Spirituality may function as a life preserver during the earlier phases of grief when you feel you are drowning.
- Spirituality may already exist in its purest form for you. For others, a much clearer concept of spiritual tenets is created during the phases of Adaptation, Equilibrium, and Transformation.
- Spirituality grows and expands over your lifetime.

LESSON 10: Create meaning from your loss.

Why:

- Because you and you alone create the meaning from your loved one's life, death, and your grief.
- Because it honors your loved one, you, and all that you have become.
- Because it transforms a tragedy into something good and beneficial through the concept of spiritual alchemy.
- Because your loved one's life and death and your grief need not have been in vain.

How:

- Through incorporating the qualities you admired in your beloved into your own personality.
- Through integrating the experience of loving and having been loved by that person.

- Through benevolent means such as organ donations, scholarships, charitable foundations, volunteering your time, energy, and money.
- Making a difference in the world through the example of your self.
- Through creative endeavors, such as painting, sculpture, music, baking bread, crafts, etc.

When:

- This is manifest in different ways throughout the phases of grief.
- During Equilibrium and Transformation, there are more resources and energy available. Hence, creating meaning is more pervasive.

LESSON 11: Exercise your sense of humor.

Why:

- Humor is one of our greatest coping mechanisms.
- Laughter and tears are authentic responses to life.
- It eases tension and provides perspective.
- It punctuates life's painful moments with restful pauses.
- It is a universal language.
- You need it for balance while grieving.

How:

- By allowing yourself to laugh without guilt and without shame.
- Through sharing memories of your loved one with friends and family.
- Through seeking out humorous resources such as movies, books, videos, etc.

When:

- Humor should be liberally applied during all phases of grief. However, it becomes easier and more natural during Equilibrium and Transformation.

LESSON 12: Help others.

Why:

- The surest way to transcend your pain and self-focus is to reach out to help someone in need.
- Helping other people is a boomerang action; you send it out and it returns to you in some benevolent way.
- You need to have a breather, and if you can't do this through hobbies or other interests, you may be able to fix your attention on helping others.
- This is something that feeds the soul and reminds you how lucky you are when looking at others' misfortunes.
- It also reminds you that you have something to give, even when you feel empty.

How:

- Through finding a need and filling it with whatever you have to spare: time, energy, or tangible items.
- Some examples include:

  reading for the blind
  driving cancer patients for treatment
  working for the Red Cross
  mentoring other grievers
  participating in a self-help group for the bereaved
  feeding the hungry
  helping the homeless
  volunteering at a battered women's shelter.

- There are thousands of places to turn your pain into something beneficial through spiritual alchemy. Go out and find them.

When:

- As soon as some excess energy is freed up from grieving.
- This is best started in the latter part of the phase of Chaos and will continue throughout the phases.
- Transformation *is* the phase of helping others.

THE GIFTS

When they embarked on their odysseys through grief, Phoenix Grievers never expected to receive anything. They only hoped that they would survive. Gradually, through amplifying their resources and developing dormant strengths, they expanded their assets. They became stronger and fuller. Over time they began to reflect on what the experience of loving, losing, and grieving had meant. And they realized that they had received many gifts through their laborious journey. One Phoenix Griever who speaks for all describes some of these gifts below.

The Gift of Courage

Grief cracked me open like an egg and challenged me beyond my imagination. I was leveled to nothingness. I had no idea that I had the guts to force myself to stand upright, take those steps forward when I didn't want to, and actually grow. When I look back I realize that it took bravery to achieve this. I took risks, tried out new behaviors, got rid of false pretenses, tried and failed, tried and succeeded, and began to trust in my own abilities. This gift continues to be an inner force that moves me past the barriers in life.

The Gift of Fellowship

I had never realized how comforting and helpful the company of others could be. They propped me up when I couldn't stand and supported my fledgling steps toward healing. They held my hand, listened, and passed me tissues when the pain spewed forth. They didn't defend themselves against my rage. They laughed with me and they cried with me. They even thought for me when my mind was numbed and temporarily out of order. They responded to my requests for help when I had the presence of mind to ask. Those who had been there made sure that they were there for me. They knew what I would be going through and what I might be needing. They made the journey less painful, less fearful, and less hopeless than it might have been. They were part of the reason I am at this point in my life. They are more than gifts; they are treasures.

The Gift of Wisdom

I thought I would gradually become old and wise when I became old. I hadn't expected to be young and wise through incongruent circumstances. Grief does that to you. After the death of a loved one, you view things and learn things differently. I skimmed over the surface of life, much like a skater over ice, never considering it from beneath the surface. I have learned about myself and my capabilities and strengths. I am learning more about my purpose in life and it has given me a direction. My loved one's life and death has adhered qualities to my personality of which I am very proud. Much of living makes more sense to me and I make sure to give my time and attention to those individuals and causes I hold dear.

The Gift of Compassion

It's not that I wasn't compassionate before; I just never paid too much attention to it. In other words, much of what I should have absorbed, I didn't. I was too caught up in life's daily agenda. I overlooked a lot of what could have touched me and brought me to another level of empathy. Now, if a person is relating some misfortune, I sort of blend with her experience and understand what it must be like for her. So for me, compassion is not co-suffering or pity; it is a deep understanding of the human experience of distress. From there, I can choose to what degree I want to involve myself to assist that person. But I have a depth of insight that I never had before.

The Gift of Being

Long before I entered grief's domain, I was absorbed in the process of becoming: becoming successful, becoming a home owner, becoming a parent, becoming financially comfortable, becoming something or other. Along with the activity of becoming, I was an expert in acquiring. It was an endless race that was impossible to win.

All that became meaningless when the one true thing, my loved one, was taken from me. I stopped becoming and acquiring and just focused on being. Death has a way of putting it all into perspective. Just being is a very nice way to live your life. It doesn't mean that you are going to become a couch potato; it means that acquiring and becoming are not the principle motivators of life.

It's all right to want to achieve, not as a goal in life, but a means to nourish and nurture your loved ones. Not to excess. Being with loved ones has become a precious commodity in this fast-paced world. I wish that this wisdom had been with me before my beloved died.

The Gift of Appreciation

Like everyone else, I took things for granted. Oh, sometimes, at some super moment I appreciated who and what were in my life, but they were more segments than an ongoing process. It's trite to say but "smelling the coffee and smelling the roses" were not priorities nor were they awarenesses once my feet hit the floor in the morning. Life is over in the blink of an eye; no one realizes that until it happens to them. Life does not wait for me or for you to appreciate what it is all about. If you miss it, then you may not have another chance to hit the rewind button.

Most of the time I am appreciative of what I have and what life has to offer. It's the natural things in life that you miss if you are not paying attention. I pay attention.

The Gift of Freedom

Life used to be filled with so many fears: fear of death, fear of life, fear of success, fear of failure, fear of snakes, and on and on in a never-ending inventory. After the death of my beloved and after facing the devastation of my world, fear seemed rather purposeless. Caution is purposeful, fear is not.

When the worst of your fears comes true, what's the purpose of fear? I found that it takes up too much time and energy to no avail. I am much more serene now. That is the irony of having suffered through the tragedy of losing a loved one. I know I have made it through and her life will not have been in vain. My grief will not have been in vain. There is no room in my world for unrealistic fears.

A major portion of this gift is the freedom to be myself. This means I choose the best for me, whether it be whom I spend time with or how I use it. It means that I can be the real me without worrying about others' reactions. Of course, with this freedom comes the responsibility to use it wisely and beneficially. I am the one who is accountable for who I am and how that manifests itself.

The Gift of Altruism

Somewhere over the course of grieving I knew that I wanted to make a difference in others' lives. I am so much more aware of what is needed by other people. It is important that I use the skills and knowledge I have received through my experiences. I see so many needs that sometimes I am overwhelmed. That is why I choose something that makes sense to me and something that I can connect with to invest my time and resources.

It is not an unselfish gesture. I receive more from making a difference in someone's life than I ever thought possible. It feels good and it makes what I have been through worthwhile.

The Gift of Spirituality

Maybe faith is a better word for this gift that I have received. It is more encompassing. When the tragedy happened, I questioned what I had been taught about a supreme being and then I destroyed the beliefs because they no longer made any sense. For the longest time I felt disconnected from anything beyond this planet. I don't know how it happened, but the hole in my soul began to fill, formless and barren at first, but gradually taking shape.

How could I have gotten to this point of healing without faith in something greater than myself? We are bound by the laws of this earthly planet and what happens, happens. What we do about it is part of our experience here. For that, we need the gift of faith in someone or something unseen. This is a very challenging concept to develop. Yet, during grief, it happened so subtly that I wasn't even consciously aware of when. I do know it is a very precious essence which I cherish.

The Gift of Love

When all is said and done and you are forced to look at what really matters in life, love is number one. Love is the essence that brought me into my journey through grief and love is the essence that fills and sustains me now. It took a while to risk loving again when the loss was so devastating. I missed love and loving. Somehow over time, I began to realize that life is hollow without love. I took the risk.

Though the journey through grief seems to be over, it continues on. The love that has been given and received in the relationship with the beloved continues to blend into the tapestry of the mourner's soul. Grief has been a valuable experience. Just how valuable is revealed at some future time, when one becomes a Phoenix Griever.

> For yesterday is but a dream,
> and tomorrow is only a vision.
> But today, well lived,
> makes every yesterday a dream of happiness,
> and every tomorrow a vision of hope.
>
> —Sanskrit proverb

And so it was that the little band of grievers realized that they would continue their journeys throughout their lives, and perhaps, beyond.

Epilogue

And it came to pass that the group of Phoenix Grievers returned to the dwelling-place of the Wise One. She greeted them warmly and rejoiced at their safe return. She prepared a welcoming feast in their honor. They were astounded that she acclaimed their endeavors and achievements.

Their leader spoke: "This honor is not deserved, O Wise One. We have done nothing remarkable. We have only repeated a journey that has been made by others who have gone before us. We have merely followed their paths."

The Wise One smiled and said, "This is true. Yet, others have not returned from their journey through grief as have you. I honor your courage and fortitude. I honor your allegiance to one another. I honor the faith and hope that has sustained you through the cave of despair. I honor the smile on your lips and the glow in your eyes."

They continued to look perplexed but felt contentment within. They partook of the banquet, and as they were eating, the Wise One asked, "Tell me of your next journey. What now?"

Puzzled, the group looked at each other. What did she mean, they asked themselves? They had just returned from their journey. One of them asked the Wise One: "What other journey is there? We have what we had sought and more. Why would we venture forth again?"

The Wise One spoke: "Yes, you have what you need. But, there are others who do not. Do you recall what I gave you to take on your odyssey?"

One of the group cried out: "Yes, you gave me a cloth for my tears."

Another spoke: "And I was given an herb for my pain."

Yet another came forth and said, "I saved my candle to protect against losing my way."

And another: "And I have the golden heart, for courage."

Then their leader spoke: "We have held each other's hands, as you have instructed, and we have tried to follow the map."

"Yes, you have what I gave you," said the Wise One. "But, there is more. Recall that other gifts were to be earned by you as you followed your guides through the passages of grief."

She continued: "You have returned from your travels wiser, more courageous, loving, and compassionate than when you left. Do you not realize that you have now become the guides? Therefore, go into the village and find those in need of direction, guidance, and hope. Give them, each from your own special gifts, what they need to return safely from their journey. As I have honored you, you will have honored your loved ones who have set you on your pilgrimage to Transformation."

And so it was that the little group of grievers set forth on another journey, this time as guides.

Resources for Therapists and Grievers: Modern Parables

METAPHORS AND GRIEF

Since the beginning of time, story telling, parables, and metaphors have conveyed deep, subconscious messages to mankind. Often, true psychological and spiritual meanings were deeply imbedded in the allegory. These messages communicated to a deeper level of the human psyche where the meaning was personalized.

Metaphors speak in a universal language, that of the human experience. Much of their power lies in their subtle, easy conveyance of information and insight through a perceptual shift.

Often, our emotions or cognitions get in the way of a particular message. Metaphors elegantly bypass the barriers and deliver their imbedded communication directly to the subconscious.

I have used metaphors in the practice of grief therapy and have found them to be remarkably effectual. One of the first was the "Fable of the Wise One and the Legos.™" This metaphor is particularly applicable in the second phase of grief, Chaos, when a mourner feels as shattered as the bereaved mother in the fable.

At the heading of each fable, I suggest a time frame in

which its use would be most relevant. For instance, the fable about the two horses would be best delivered at the time when grief needs to be expressed and an individual may be reluctant to do so.

Many people are more comfortable with story telling or delivering a message through the vehicle of a parable. Some are not. As with everything in life, this choice is personal, unique, and reflective of the person's personality. It is also helpful to let the griever read a fable. Metaphors may be used by both therapists and non-therapists alike. I offer this collection of parables as additional resources.

This is a fable for phase one, Impact, which describes the stunned and shattered feelings of the griever and the destruction of a way of life that was lived before the loss.

THE PARABLE OF THE LEGOS™

And it came to pass that the grieving mother went to the Wise One to seek comfort and hope in the aftermath of her child's death. "What is it that you want of me?" she asked.

"That you offer me a sign of hope that there will be healing from my painful wounds of grief," answered the grieving mother "and that you assure me that I am not damaged beyond repair."

The Wise One was filled with compassion for the grieving woman and she replied, "Go home to your child's room, and take from his box of toys his Lego building blocks. Build a magnificent house from the pieces and bring it to me."

Bewildered and uncertain, the grieving mother did as the Wise One directed. She spent many days and nights in the room of her son. Through her tears, sleeplessness, and heartache, she built an impressive Lego structure. Exhausted and depleted, yet relieved and proud of her creation, she brought it to the Wise One.

Holding the grieving mother's completed task in her hands, the Wise One said, "This is indeed a magnificent structure of much effort and labor." Whereupon she raised it high overhead and dashed it to the ground, where it shattered into hundreds of pieces.

The grieving mother could not believe her eyes. She was shocked, confused, outraged, and heartbroken. "I came to you for comfort and hope, O Wise One, and you have cruelly destroyed my expectations. My hope lies fragmented and shattered, as is this structure."

The Wise One reached down to the distraught mother and held her in a comforting embrace. She then knelt on the ground and picked up every tiny Lego piece. All were intact, save one, which was cracked and damaged, yet of value to the whole. The Wise One placed the pieces in a golden treasure box and handed it to the grieving mother.

"These are the fragments of your being. Every piece is here. Not one is unaccounted for. Take them and use every one to create a new dwelling. For even the cracked and damaged piece, which has sustained grievous injury, has prevailed. It has earned the place of honor. It shall be the cornerstone of your structure. And so shall your being be made whole and complete again in a new configuration. Go now and begin to rebuild," directed the Wise One.

The grieving woman left, carrying her golden treasure box and the jumbled pieces of Legos. She went home and began the long and arduous task of rebuilding a new and magnificent abode. And so it was as the Wise One foretold.

This is a fable for phases one and two, Impact and Chaos, describing grief as a "familiar stranger."

THE PARABLE OF THE MALADIES

And it came to pass that a group of grievers ascended the mountain to the dwelling of the Wise One. As it was in those days, those seeking solace and enlightenment when distraught willingly made the treacherous journey. Thus, from the valley came the seekers.

The Wise One welcomed the weary travelers and asked, "How may I serve you?" The leader replied, "A strange malady has befallen this wretched group you see before you, an ailment with which we have no familiarity or remedy. We beseech your advice."

"Tell me of this affliction. At what time did it begin and what are its manifestations?" asked the Wise One.

A young man stepped forward and replied, "It feels like there is a large rock pressing against my throat so it is difficult to swallow and hence I cannot eat very much. And a bizarre fire of anger roars through my blood and disturbs my mind and body. I noticed it soon after my mother and father succumbed to the fever that raged through our village."

An old, wizened woman with gnarled hands spoke. "I, too, have a tightness in my throat that is sometimes relieved by shedding tears. It began when my dear husband, companion of fifty years, fell victim to the same infirmity."

Another stepped forward. "My child also died, in my arms, of the same fever. My chest began to ache constantly as if I had an ague. It will not go away."

On and on it went as all related their ailments to the Wise One. Finally, the last one related her story. "The place where my heart resides feels as heavy as a boulder, yet very empty. It aches as if it had taken a grievous blow. But it has not.

What can these peculiarities be?" she said.

The Wise One invited them to walk outside with her to the edge of the mountain that overlooked their beautiful valley. She then spoke: "This malady of which you speak is not an unfamiliar one. Each of you has felt aspects of it in your lifetime."

She took the hand of the old, wizened woman, looked into her eyes and said, "Many years ago, when you left your dear parents' abode and wed your husband you suffered the same malady. It is called grief."

She turned to the young man whose parents had died and said, "Last year, part of your crops were damaged through a fire set through the carelessness of one of your laborers. You felt the same misery as you do now. It is called grief."

To each member of the group she responded and explained that their distress was natural and familiar and was the aftermath of suffering a loss. "This natural event is greatly intensified when one's loved one has died," she said.

And to the young woman with the heavy yet empty heart, she counseled, "Soon the heaviness and emptiness will balance and you will find relief from your anguish. Have faith and hope, for you have healed before from this mystery called grief and you will again."

The Wise One embraced and blessed each weary traveler and bade them safe passage through the journey of grief. And so it was that the group of grievers was comforted. They left, feeling confident in their ability to heal from the puzzling sensations that were no longer unfamiliar.

This is a fable for phase two, Chaos, in which the need for expression of feelings and grief work is advised.

THE PARABLE OF THE TWO HORSES

And it came to pass that an old man approached the Wise One to seek a solution to a distressing situation. She led him into her dwelling place and asked him why he had come.

He bowed his head in sorrow and spoke: "My son is in deep emotional pain and sorrow. He moves as if he were in a trance. I cannot bear to see him this way. How can I restore him to as he was before? How can I end his anguish? Please help me, O Wise One."

The Wise One asked the man what had caused this strangeness in his son. The old man responded, "My son married late in life to a woman so sweet and good that he never regretted the years of waiting. Last month she and their infant died in childbirth. My son is no longer as he was. I need to stop his suffering at once and put his grief to rest."

Pondering the old man's request, the Wise One went to the door overlooking a verdant meadow. Wildflowers glowed in the sun and horses pranced about. She beckoned to him and said, "Observe the horses in the field. That one who romps and plays with the tiny foal suffered a severe injury to her leg. She cried and moaned and screamed in outrage and pain, then settled down for a long while to rest and heal. Now she is stronger than before."

She motioned toward another horse that was lying down, appearing to be resting. "Observe there, in the other corner of the meadow, the horse that is not prancing about. He also severely injured his leg. He ignored the injury to this vital part and ran and pranced as if nothing had happened. As a consequence of this denial of his injury he is damaged and lame. He can no longer keep up with the other horses, nor has he the desire."

The old man stared at the horses for a long while, reflecting on the meaning of this story. Tears rolled down his cheeks as he turned to the Wise One and said: "I understand. Thank you." She embraced him and bade him safe passage home.

Upon returning to the village, the old man went to his son's home and shared what he had learned. The young man felt a stirring of hope beneath the pain and smiled at his father. The old man encouraged and supported his son's natural expressions of grief. And so it was that the young man emerged from his trance and began to heal.

This is a fable for phase two, Chaos, which suggests that grief's wounds need not be seen to be felt.

THE PARABLE OF THE INVISIBLE WOUND

And it came to pass that a grieving father climbed the steep terrain that led to the dwelling of the Wise One. With hands over his heart and his body bent over with pain he asked for relief and enlightenment. "My heart feels as if a knife were thrust into it. I feel so sick that I cannot eat or sleep as I once did. I cannot understand why the pain is so intense, for no one has injured or stabbed me. I implore you, O Wise One, help me with this suffering. Help me to understand this enigma."

The Wise One assisted the grieving father to a chair and asked, "Tell me, sir, when was it that you first felt this pain?" Slowly, he gathered his thoughts to form a clear answer. Finally, he spoke. "The mysterious pain came upon me a long while after my young daughter died of a malady of the blood. I had no pain when she died. It was as if I were frozen in a block of ice. But later I was wracked with this anguish. How can an injury this painful not be visible?"

The Wise One pondered this question for a long while. She sat beside the man, took his hand, and began to speak. "Many years ago, a calamitous earthquake came to a nearby land and visited much devastation and destruction upon the land and its people. Many huts fell into crevasses and scores of villagers died. It was a catastrophe that was witnessed by the dwellers who survived.

"Now the very earth was so shaken that the air around it grew agitated and violent. An invisible force gathered and sent out its destructive power to the land and to its people who were many, many distances away. This unseen energy caused wounds and pain in those innocent victims who had no knowledge of the earthquake."

The Wise One looked gently upon the suffering man and continued, "A calamity which causes serious damage need not be seen, nor wounds be evident to prove that serious injury has occurred, as it was with the death of your daughter. The magnitude of the shock waves caused harm and pain as surely as if someone had thrust a knife through your heart. Know that the wound will heal over time if you treat it as if it were a lesion you could see and touch."

The father grasped both hands of the Wise One and spoke: "Thank you. I understand that my pain is as it should be from this terrible misfortune. I will do as you say." He then returned to the village to begin healing.

This is a fable for phases two and three, Chaos and Adaptation, which speaks of the failure of old beliefs to support the reality of the death of a loved one.

THE PARABLE OF LEGENDS AND BELIEFS

And it came to pass that a company of farmers journeyed to the dwelling place of the Wise One. Their homes and crops had been destroyed by an inferno of extraordinary magnitude. Many had lost their wives and children. Their farmlands were in ashes. They came seeking wisdom and guidance in their grief.

The Wise One welcomed them into her home, where they began explaining the reasons for their pilgrimage.

"Our lives had been built according to the beliefs of our ancestors and in our trust in the ways of the Almighty Spirit. We believed that if we were good people, good things would come back to us. We worked hard and were good to our families and others but destruction has been our reward. Yet, there were others who were not good people and yet their families are safe. What sense does this make for what we had been taught to believe?"

The Wise One considered this question, one that had been asked for many decades and answered thusly: "There is a vast difference between legends passed unto you and your own beliefs. One comes from the mouths and hearts of others but the truth grows from within your own hearts and souls. Living a good life does not prevent disasters from affecting you, nor does it protect those whom you call 'not good people.' Unnatural acts that cause suffering and death are natural occurrences in our lives. They are neither rewards nor punishments. They are merely the happenings of this life."

"What then is the place of the Almighty?" asked one farmer.

The Wise One replied, "The Almighty is your Creator, your friend, your enemy, your judge, your helpmate, your guide, whatever you and you alone believe."

The farmer pondered the answer and replied, "I believe that the Almighty allows me to choose my ways in life and stands by to guide me."

Another came forth and said, "I believe that the Almighty is my own reflection in the heavens and this is how I judge my own goodness."

A third farmer stepped forward and said, "I believe that my Almighty One loves all and judges not, nor does He punish. He comforts us and gives us strength in our sorrow."

Many of the group were astonished at these sayings and one spoke to the Wise One. "We have never heard these beliefs before, but they feel better than our old ones."

"Yes, it is so," said the Wise One. "By these feelings in your heart and soul you will come to know your own beliefs."

The Wise One then asked if she could offer any other thoughts on their woes. One young farmer stepped forward. "And what of our land, which is scorched and barren where once we had fields of golden wheat?" he asked.

The Wise One responded, "The ashes and your beliefs are one. That which forms the foundation of your lives is still there upon which to build. For the sun shines on your land, the rains come to nourish it, and from the ashes of the earth will arise new growth. Where there once was wheat there will be corn, and where there once were weeds there will be flowers, and the cycles of life will go on. These beliefs are true and unchanging. Upon these will you build your own."

The farmers looked at the Wise One and at each other with new understanding and the seeds of new faith in their souls. They thanked her, bade her farewell, and returned to their village to begin the regeneration of the earth from the ashes.

This is a fable for the third phase of grief, Adaptation, which addresses the need for hope even when the pain seems to be interminable.

THE PARABLE OF THE CAVE OF DARKNESS

And it came to pass that a group of grievers sought wisdom and guidance of the Wise One. They were a weary and suffering parcel of souls looking for fortitude to continue their journey through grief.

"You are welcome in my dwelling," said the Wise One. She prepared a place of rest and refreshment and then listened to the accounts of their sorrows. One of the group spoke: "Many months ago, we were content with our lots in life. Our crops were bountiful, our children fed, and our spouses safeguarded. Then, the river that had nurtured us for so long became swollen with the storms of summer and overflowed into our valley. That night, as we slept, the powerful currents swept away the loved ones belonging to this woeful group you see before you. Our children, our spouses, our belongings, our dwellings, all lost! From the depths of the darkness of our souls we wonder if despair is to be our fate for the rest of our lives."

The Wise One heard the pain and hopelessness beneath their words and began to tell a story. "Many decades ago, a caravan of sojourners fled their harsh, infertile land to seek a land of bounty. For many weeks they traveled over treacherous terrain hoping to reach a better place in which to live.

"One day the travelers reached an impasse where they could go no farther. A wall of rock that was too steep to climb and too wide to go around blocked their way. A large dark hole in the rock indicated a cave which the group decided to enter, hoping to pass through to their destination.

"For several days they walked through the cave with only minimal light twinkling from small openings far above, until they came to the place where no light could enter. From the depths of their despair a great conflict arose.

"Many wanted to go back to their arid land. Others wanted to move forward, hopeful that they would emerge from the cave. There were those who were so fearful and without hope that they wanted to remain there in the darkness. Finally, those with courage and determination pushed onward and emerged on the other side into a better place."

"And what of the others?" asked one of the grievers.

The Wise One replied, "Some went back to their old way of life in the harsh land. Those without hope remain in the cave of darkness for they do not believe there is anything beyond." She then left the group alone for awhile to ponder the message of the story.

The members of the assemblage sat and pondered the meaning of the Wise One's tale. Some time later they felt enlightened and felt the stirrings of hope within their souls. With immense gratitude and appreciation, they took their leave of the Wise One and made their way back to the valley with renewed zeal.

This is a fable for the fourth and fifth phases, Equilibrium and Transformation, in which different outcomes of grief are described.

THE PARABLE OF THE THREE FARMERS

And it came to pass that a group of grievers celebrated their safe return to their village and hastened up the mountainside to the dwelling place of the Wise One. She greeted them warmly and they sat around the fire and talked companionably for many hours. As darkness fell, they asked her about other travelers and of their passages through grief. They wondered if all had returned as had they, in a wondrous manner.

She fell silent for a long while, then turned to the little group and began to tell them a story. "A long while ago, in your very own village, there were three prosperous farmers whose crops were lush and bountiful and greatly admired by the villagers. These were times of abundance and the rhythm of nature was unaltered for many decades. And so it was that the silos and storehouses of the farmers were full and brimming with grain and seed and harvest.

"And then the nature of the seasons shifted and the earth was not fertile enough to nourish the crops that year. The farmers' fields lay fallow, as did their neighbors'. Famine and hardship fell across the land.

"The first of the three farmers ate well but shared none of his bounty. He hid what he had in the darkness of his cellarplace. Time passed and the grain began to sour and decay and the rodents took the rest and there was waste and more deprivation.

"The second farmer also ate well and fed his family equally as well. He did not hide his bounty but kept its whereabouts and existence to himself. They were sustained and nurtured until the earth once again provided sustenance to the crops.

"The third farmer fed himself and his family. Then, he ventured forth to his neighbors and others in the village to share his grain and produce so that others might be fed and have enough to plant when the earth was ready to receive the seed. From his plentiful harvest many were nourished and many more crops were regenerated. Thus was his harvest multiplied, generation after generation."

She paused and looked at the group of grievers.

They spoke not a word, but took the story into their hearts and applied it to their own lives. And so it was that from them, many were nurtured, generation after generation.

And so it is that this part of the passage comes to a close for the Phoenix Grievers and a passage begins for future Phoenix Grievers.

Appendix

There are two valuable resources for further reading on death loss and grief: Compassion Books and The Compassionate Friends, Inc. Their lists are very extensive, comprehensive, and appropriate for grievers, therapists, and other helpers. Both offer mail-order services.

Compassion Books
477 Hannah Branch Rd.
Burnsville, NC 28714
Phone: (704) 675-5909
Fax: (704) 675-9687
www.compassionbooks.com

The Compassionate Friends, Inc.
P.O. Box 3696
Oak Brook, IL 60522-3696
Phone (630) 990-0010
Fax: (603) 990-0246

References

Allport, G. W. (1969). Preface. In *Man's Search for Meaning*, ed. V. E. Frankl, pp. ix–xv. New York: Washington Square Press.

American Heritage Dictionary (1979). Boston: Houghton Mifflin.

American Psychiatric Association (1994). *Diagnostic and Statistical Manual of Mental Disorders*, 4th ed. Washington, DC: Author.

Andreas, C., and Andreas, S. (1989). *Heart of the Mind*. Moab, UT: Real People Press.

Benoliel, J. O. (1985). Loss and adaptation. *Death Studies* 9:217–233.

Bess, J., and Bartlett, G. E. (1974). Creative grief. In *Death and Bereavement*, ed. A. Kutscher, 2nd printing, pp. 317–318. Springfield, IL: Charles C Thomas.

Bowlby, J. (1961). Processes of mourning. *International Journal of Psycho-Analysis* 42(4–5):317–340.

Calhoun, L. G., and Tedeschi, R. G. (1989–1990). Positive aspects of critical life problems: recollections of grief. *OMEGA, Journal of Death and Dying* 21:265–272.

Casarjian, R. (1992). *Forgiveness: A Bold Choice for a Peaceful Heart*. New York: Bantam.

Cassem, N. H. (1975). Bereavement as indispensable for growth. In *Bereavement: Its Psychosocial Aspects*, ed. B. Schoenberg et al., pp. 9–17. New York: Columbia University Press.

Eisenstadt, J. M. (1978). Parental loss and genius. *American Psychologist*, March, pp. 211–223.

Engel, G. L. (1961). Is grief a disease? *Psychosomatic Medicine* 23:18–22.

Higgins, G. (1994). *Resilient Adults: Overcoming a Cruel Past*. San Francisco: Jossey-Bass.

Holmes, T. H., and Rahe, R. H. (1967). Social readjustment rating scale. *Journal of Psychosomatic Research* 2:213–218.

Jackson, E. N. (1961). *You and Your Grief*. New York: Channel.

―――― (1977). *The Many Faces of Grief*. Nashville: Abingdon.

James, J. (1988). *Women and the Blues: Passions that Hurt, Passions that Heal*. San Francisco: Harper & Row.

Kastenbaum, R. J. (1986). *Death, Society and Human Experience*, 3rd ed. Columbus, OH: Charles E. Merrill.

Koontz, D. (1996). *Beautiful Death*, ed. D. Robinson. New York: Penguin.

Kushner, H. (1981). *When Bad Things Happen to Good People*. New York: Schocken.

Lindemann, E. (1944). Symptomatology and management of acute grief. *American Journal of Psychiatry* 101:141–148.

Mahler, M. (1961). On sadness and grief in infancy and childhood. *Psychoanalytic Study of the Child* 16. New York: International Universities Press.

Maslow, A. (1968). *Toward a Psychology of Being*, 2nd ed. New York: Van Nostrand.

―――― (1970). *Motivation and Personality*, 2nd ed. New York: Harper & Row.

―――― (1987). *Motivation and Personality*, 3rd ed. New York: Harper & Row.

Moriarty, D. M., ed. (1967). *The Loss of Loved Ones*. Springfield, IL: Charles C Thomas.

Parkes, C. M. (1971). Psychosocial transitions: a field for study. *Social Science and Medicine* 5:101–115.

―――― (1972). *Bereavement: Studies of Grief in Adult Life*, 3rd ed. New York: International Universities Press.

Pennebacker, J. W. (1990). *The Healing Power of Expressing Emotions*. New York: Guilford.

Petri, H. L. (1981). *Motivation: Theory, Research and Applications*, 3rd ed. Belmont, CA: Wadsworth.

Rando, T. A. (1988). *Grieving: How to Go on Living When Someone You Love Dies*. Lexington, MA: Lexington Books.

———— (1993). *Treatment of Complicated Mourning*. Champaign, IL: Research Press.

Raphael, B. (1983). *The Anatomy of Bereavement*. New York: Basic Books.

Ratey, J. J., and Johnson, C. (1997). *Shadow Syndromes*. New York: Pantheon.

Sanders, C. M. (1989). *Grief: The Mourning After*. New York: Wiley.

Siebert, A. (1996). *The Survivor Personality*. New York: Berkeley.

Simonton, O. C., Mathews-Simonton, S., and Creighton, J. (1978). *Getting Well Again*. Los Angeles, CA: J. P. Tarcher.

Stroebe, W., and Stroebe, M. S. (1987). Bereavement and Health. *The Psychological and Physical Consequences of Partner Loss.* Cambridge, England: Cambridge University Press.

Tedeschi, R. G., and Calhoun, L. G. (1995). *Trauma and Transformation*. Thousand Oaks, CA: Sage.

Viorst, J. (1986). *Necessary Losses*. New York: Fawcett Columbine.

Worden, W. J. (1991). *Grief Counseling and Grief Therapy: A Handbook for the Mental Health Practitioner*, 2nd ed. New York: Springer.

Supportive Literature

Abrams, J. L. (1981). Depression versus normal grief following the death of a significant other. In *New Directions in Cognitive Therapy: A Casebook*, ed. C. Emery, pp. 255–270. New York: Guilford.

Aquilera, D. C., and Messick, J. M. (1974). *Crisis Intervention, Theory and Methodology*. St. Louis: Mosby.

Braun, M. J., and Dale, H. (1994). Meaning reconstruction in the experience of parental bereavement. *Death Studies* 18:105–129.

Bullitt, D. (1996). *Filling the Void*. New York: Rawson Associates.

Burns, D. (1980). *Feeling Good: The New Mood Therapy*. New York: William Morrow.

Calhoun, L. G., Selby, J. W., and King, H. E. (1976). *Dealing with Crisis: A Guide to Critical Life Problems*. Englewood Cliffs, NJ: Prentice Hall.

Cousins, N. (1989). *Head First: The Biology of Hope*. New York: Dutton.

Das, S. S. (1971). Grief and suffering. In *Psychotherapy: Theory, Research and Practice* 8(1):8–9, Spring.

Edelman, H. (1994). *Motherless Daughters*. New York: Delta.

Ellis, A. (1981). The rational emotive approach to thanatology. In *Behavior Therapy in Terminal Care: A Humanistic Approach*, ed. H. Sobel, pp. 151–176. Cambridge, MA: Ballinger.

Fitzgerald, H. (1994). *The Mourning Handbook*. New York: Simon & Schuster.

Fleming, S., and Robinson, P. J. (1991). The application of cognitive therapy to the bereaved. In *The Challenge of Cognitive Therapy: Applications to Nontraditional Populations*, ed. T. M. Vallis and J. L. Howes, pp. 135–158. New York: Plenum.

Frank, A. (1991). *At the Will of the Body*. New York: Harper & Row.

Frankl, V. E. (1969). *Man's Search for Meaning*. New York: Washington Square Press.

Freeman, L. (1978). *The Sorrow and the Fury*. Englewood Cliffs, NJ: Prentice Hall.

Gauthier, J., and Marshal, W. L. (1977). Grief: a cognitive-behavioral analysis. *Cognitive Therapy and Research* 1(1):39–44.

Gibran, K. (1923). *The Prophet*. New York: Knopf.

Glasser, W. (1975). *Reality Therapy*. New York: Harper & Row.

Glick, I. O., Weiss, R. S., and Parkes, C. M. (1974). *The First Year of Bereavement*. New York: Wiley.

Graham, B. (1991). *Hope for the Troubled Heart*. Dallas: World.

Grollman, E. A., ed. (1981). *What Helped Me When My Loved One Died*. Boston: Beacon.

Guidan, V. F., and Liotto, G. (1983). *Cognitive Processes and Emotional Disorders*. New York: Guilford.

Hammarskjold, D. (1964). *Markings*. New York: Knopf.

Hammen, C., and Mayol, A. (1982). Depression and cognitive characteristics of stressful life-events. *Journal of Abnormal Psychology* 1:165–174.

Harris, M. (1995). *The Loss That Is Forever*. New York: Penguin.

Kessler, B. G. (1987). Bereavement and personal growth. *Journal of Humanistic Psychology* 7(2):228–247.

Krauth, L. D. (1995). Strength based therapies. *Family Therapy News* December, 26:24.

Kübler-Ross, E. (1969). *On Death and Dying*. Toronto: Macmillan.

Kutscher, A. H., ed. (1974). *Death and Bereavement*, 2nd ed. Springfield, IL: Charles C Thomas.

Landorf, J. (1974). *Mourning Song*. Old Tappan, NJ: Fleming H. Renell.

Lazare, A. (1979). Unresolved grief. In *Outpatient Psychiatry: Diagnosis and Treatment*, pp. 498–512. Baltimore: Williams & Wilkins.

Lehman, D. R., Wortman, C. B., and Williams, A. F. (1987). Long-term effects of losing a spouse or child in a motor vehicle crash. In *Journal of Personality and Social Psychology* 52(1):218–231.

Lindbergh, A. M. (1973). *Hour of Gold, Hour of Lead*. New York: Harcourt Brace.

Lindemann, E. (1979). *Beyond Grief*. New York: Jason Aronson.

Lewis, C. S. (1994). *A Grief Observed*. San Francisco: HarperCollins.

Margolis, O. S., Raether, H. C., Kutscher, A. H., et al., eds. (1981). *Acute Grief: Counseling the Bereaved*. New York: Columbia University Press.

Maslow, A. (1954). *Motivation and Personality*. New York: Harper & Row.

Masson, J. M., and McCarthy, S. (1995). *When Elephants Weep: The Emotional Lives of Animals*. New York: Delta.

Mathers, J. (1974). The gestation period of identity change. *British Journal of Psychiatry* 125:472–474.

Miles, M. S., and Crandal, E. K. (1983). The search for meaning and its potential for affecting growth in bereaved parents. *Health Values: Achieving High Level Wellness* 2(1):19–23.

Mosteller, B. A., ed. (1983). Cognitive psychology: a method for exploring death's "gifts." *Health Values: Achieving High Level Wellness* 7(1):44–47.

Nerken, I. R. (1993). Grief and the reflective self: toward a clearer model of loss resolution and growth. *Death Studies* 17:21–26.

Nuland, S. (1993). *How We Die*. New York: Knopf.

O'Connor, N. (1984). *Letting Go with Love: The Grieving Process*. Apache Junction, AZ: La Mariposa.

Parkes, C. M. (1988). Bereavement as a psychosocial transition: processes of adaptation to change. *Journal of Social Issues* 44(3):53–65.

Pollock, G. H. (1961). Mourning and adaptation. *International Journal of Psycho-Analysis* 42:341–361.

——— (1977). The mourning process and creative organizational change. *Journal of the American Psychoanalytic Association* 25(1):3–34.

Prend, A. D. (1997). *Transcending Loss*. New York: Berkley.

Rando, T. A. (1984). *Grief, Dying and Death*. Champaign, IL: Research Press.

——— (1986). *Loss and Anticipatory Grief*. Lexington, MA: D. C. Heath.

Ramsey, R. W. (1977). Behavioural approaches to bereavement. *Behaviour Research and Therapy* 15: 131–135.

Rubin, S. S. (1984–1985). Maternal attachment and child death: on adjustment, relationship, and resolution. *OMEGA* 15(4):347–352.

Schiff, H. S. (1977). *The Bereaved Parent*. New York: Crown.

——— (1986). *Living Through Mourning*. New York: Viking Penguin.

Schneider, J. M. (1980). Clinically significant differences between grief, pathological grief and depression. *Patient Counseling and Health Education*, fourth quarter, pp. 161–169.

Schoenberg, B., Gerber, I., Wiener, A., et al. eds. (1975). *Bereavement: Its Psychosocial Aspects*. New York: Columbia University Press.

Seligman, M. E. P. (1990). *Learned Optimism*. New York: Pocket Books.

Sheehy, G. (1995). *New Passages*. New York: Ballantine.

Siegel, B. S. (1986). *Love, Medicine and Miracles*. New York: Harper & Row.

Silverman, W. B., and Cinnamon, K. (1990). *When Mourning Comes: A Book of Comfort for the Grieving*. Northvale, NJ: Jason Aronson.

Simos, B. G. (1977). Grief therapy to facilitate healthy restitution. *Social Casework*, June, pp. 337–342.

Solari-Wadell, P. A., Schmidt-Bunkers, S., Chin, E., and Snyder, D. (1995). The pinwheel model of bereavement. *Image: Journal of Nursing Scholarship* 27:323–326.

Stadacher, C. (1987). *Beyond Grief*. Oakland, CA: New Harbinger.

Tansley, T. (1995). *For Women Who Grieve*. Freedom, CA: The Crossing Press.

Taylor, S. E. (1983). Adjustment to threatening events: a theory of cognitive adaptation. *American Psychologist*, November, pp. 1161–1173.

Viscott, D. (1976). *The Language of Feelings*. New York: Pocket Books.

Wahl, C. W. (1970). The differential diagnosis of normal and neurotic grief following bereavement. *Psychosomatics* 11(2):104–106.

Yapko, M. D. (1988). *When Living Hurts*. New York: Brunner/Mazel.

Index